CORRIE

The Lives She's Touched

BY Joan Winmill Brown
No Longer Alone
Day by Day With Billy Graham
Wings of Joy
Every Knee Shall Bow
Corrie: The Lives She's Touched

Corrie
The Lives She's Touched

Joan Winmill Brown

Fleming H. Revell Company
Old Tappan, New Jersey

Scripture quotations identified KJV are from the King James Version of the Bible.

Scripture quotations identified PHILLIPS are from THE NEW TESTAMENT IN MODERN ENGLISH (Revised Edition), translated by J. B. Phillips. © J. B. Phillips 1958, 1960, 1972. Used by permission of the Macmillan Publishing Co., Inc.

Scripture quotations identified NAS are from the New American Standard Bible, Copyright © THE LOCKMAN FOUNDATION 1960, 1962, 1963, 1968, 1971, 1972, 1973, 1975 and are used by permission.

We are indebted to a number of sources for the photographs in this volume. We especially want to thank Russ Busby, who took so many photographs of Corrie over the years. Our gratitude, too, to World Wide Pictures for the use of the photographs from the film *The Hiding Place,* and to Hans Poley, who provided the photographs taken at the Beje during the Nazi occupation.

Library of Congress Cataloging in Publication Data

Brown, Joan Winmill.
    Corrie, the lives she's touched.

    Includes index.
    1. Ten Boom, Corrie. 2. Christian biography--
Netherlands. I. Title.
BR1725.T35B76   269'.2'0924 [B]   79-20893
ISBN 0-8007-1049-5
ISBN 0-8007-1050-9 pbk.

At the time I was writing this book, Corrie ten Boom was gravely ill, and each day I did not know if she would go to be with the Lord. The question arose as to what tense I should use.

As I wrote about Corrie's life, I realized once more that, whatever happened, she would always be with us in spirit and example, because of Jesus Christ.

Since, for Corrie—as for each of us who know Him—heaven is a continuation of living, I have written this book in the present tense.

This book is lovingly dedicated to the memory of the courageous ten Boom family of Haarlem, Holland.

J.W.B.

Contents

Preface

When I was first asked to write this book about Corrie ten Boom, I wondered, "Hasn't everything already been written about this incredible lady?" Then I flew to Holland and began researching—visiting places where Corrie's story had been lived, meeting with people from out of her past—and I was absolutely entranced. *Volumes* could still be written about Corrie, especially about the lives she has touched.

When I arrived in Haarlem, Corrie's hometown, it was a cold, freezing, rainy day, but the colorful architecture and the personality of this thriving market town captured my imagination. As I walked up her street, the Barteljorisstraat, my mind went back into the past. Standing by the bakery opposite the narrow, quaint, Dutch house that had belonged to the ten Booms, I could visualize Papa ten Boom coming to the door of his watch shop to greet his customers. I imagined Betsie arriving on her bicycle, ladened with groceries—Corrie opening the side door to help her, and their laughing together, enjoying the moment.

My mind then flashed to a different scene—down the cobblestone streets came the thunder of German tanks and goose-stepping Nazi soldiers. From that same little peaceful house I could see the ten Booms led away to prison by the Gestapo. . . .

Returning to the present scene around me, I saw children laughing and playing in the rain, shoppers gossiping, and the very same brightly painted street organ (drawn by a gaily bedecked horse) that Corrie would have known as a child, playing a haunting Schubert melody.

I thought, *Do these people have any idea of what actually took place in the house across the street; the Jews that were saved; the suffering of the ten Booms; their undaunted faith in Christ?*

Perhaps some of the older people might remember, but the price of freedom—which is so often taken for granted—is one that is paid so that future generations can live in peace.

This book is one over which I have prayed, as I have written each chapter, that while being a tribute to Corrie, it might, above all, glorify the Christ she loves. This book is a testimony, a hymn of praise, as it were, to our Lord Jesus. Like Corrie, if we really take Him at His word and believe that He is with us always, then nothing that is evil in this life can conquer us.

There are many lessons to be learned from the courageous ten Booms, among them, the value of a consecrated Christian home and the joy—the absolute joy—of serving our Lord with the strength that *He* gives through His Word.

In writing this book the Lord gave me such wonderful help in the person of Margaret Gabel. I want to thank her, together with Pamela Rosewell, Lotte Reimeringer, Bettie Butler, and Ron Rietveld for their assistance.

Especially, my thanks go to our Lord for the privilege of being able to bring to the public more inspiring stories of a very special child of His, Corrie ten Boom.

JOAN WINMILL BROWN

Corrie's birth certificate.

Corrie with Billy Graham.

Saint Bavo's Cathedral.

Interior of the magnificent
Saint Bavo's Cathedral.

The majestic organ in Saint Bavo's
Cathedral which Corrie and her
family enjoyed listening to.

Introduction

This is one of the most amazing lives of the century! It constantly shows how God's grace and love can sustain us in the worst of times. Corrie ten Boom and her family stood up for persons in a minority group—the Jews. It cost most of them their lives. It is amazing how these Dutch Christians speak to all of us in our world, our society, our lives today.

Corrie ten Boom's story has a strong message for Christians. The greatest need in the church today is to realize that judgment is coming, troubles are coming, and we must have disciplined, hardy Christian lives. This is the example of the experience of Corrie ten Boom and her family—of Christian lives disciplined by the Word of God and the power of His Spirit giving strength and courage to fight evil and to triumph over it!

BILLY GRAHAM

On April 15, 1892, the bells of the majestic fifteenth-century Cathedral of Saint Bavo pealed out their magnificent melody, awakening the residents of Haarlem, Holland.

To most of the citizens, as they sleepily began their daily tasks, it was just another ordinary morning. Little did they know that a baby girl was to be born that day whose life would touch, in such a lasting way, so many of their lives and others throughout the world.

As a little child, she would touch lives with her prayers. As she grew, her teachings and compassion would reach out to anyone in need. The mentally retarded would be especially loved by her. For the Jewish people, she would suffer, along with her sister Betsie, the horror of a concentration camp. Even in that man-made hell, she would be used by the Lord to bring hope and comfort to all those around her. Eventually, after being released, her travels, her books, and her films would communicate to millions a lesson so intensely learned: that "no pit is so deep that God's love is not deeper still."

11

Her story is one of a woman who, in every circumstance, no matter how old she has grown, has never lost her childlike faith in a Savior—who not only died for her salvation—but is One who lives and walks with her each day.

The name given to her at birth was Cornelia Arnolda Johanna ten Boom—but to the countless thousands who love her, she is known simply and most affectionately as: Corrie.

On the morning of her birth, the local newspaper, the *Haarlems Dagblad,* ran articles about the young Kaiser Wilhelm II, who later would lead Germany into World War I. There was news of other world leaders—the Khedive of Egypt, a Russian diplomat, the Emperor of China. It also told of the young Princess Wilhelmina, who in a few years would ascend the throne. One day her daughter, Juliana, would honor Corrie ten Boom by knighting her for heroism in World War II. There would be a warm friendship between these two women, Wilhelmina and Corrie—socially so far apart, yet with the same need in their lives: to be loved and forgiven by Jesus Christ.

Corrie ten Boom's life, her total forgiveness of and love for her enemies have amazed all who have met her. What is her secret? Why is she known around the world, honored in nation after nation, and loved by so many hundreds whose lives she has touched?

The world is hungry and Corrie has given it food—the kind for which it is starving—food for the spirit. The explanation for all that her life has become is found in Romans 5:5 (NAS):

> . . . the love of God has been poured out within our
> hearts through the Holy Spirit who was given to us.

Corrie was willing to embody His love, to interpret it into life, regardless of the cost. Corrie has said, "If you give room in your heart for the Holy Spirit, He will give you *His* love, a part of the fruit of the Spirit—and that love never fails."

To understand how God prepared this incredible woman so that she could be used to bring His message of Love, we must go back to her humble beginnings. . . .

CORRIE
The Lives She's Touched

1

"A Grain of Wheat"

Early ten Boom family photo (Corrie, left front).

The baby was cradled in her mother's arms, just a tiny wad of life. She was born prematurely, and the doctor wondered whether she would live. Her uncle prayed that the Lord might take this little life to be with Him, for surely it would be more merciful for this pathetic little creature to be spared the struggle that she would have to face in order to live.

Her mother smiled as she looked down into those beautiful vivid-blue eyes. With a heart full of love, she thanked the Lord for this new addition to the family.

The young father, leaning over the bed, instinctively prayed that his little "grain of wheat" might live and bring forth much fruit for the kingdom of God. He prayed this often for all his children—it came naturally to him, for his life was completely devoted to his Savior.

Such love surrounded the new child, it seemed to give her a determination to live. Her brother, Willem, sisters Betsie and Nollie welcomed the little baby into their lives. As Corrie grew into a happy, healthy child, their house resounded with her laughter.

The devoted Dutch family lived over their little watch shop, called the Beje. It was situated on the busy Barteljorisstraat, only yards away from the Grote Markt (the marketplace). This cobbled street, teeming with life, and the narrow alley at the side of their shop would have to serve as a playground for the ten Boom children. But they were happy, because their whole world revolved around parents who had made the Beje a dedicated, loving home.

Papa ten Boom was greatly loved by the citizens of Haarlem. A truly venerable patriarch with his long beard, he greeted everyone as they passed by. For him there was always time for kindness, defending the oppressed. In difficulty they would always come to him.

He was a great man of prayer, bringing the problem of a stubborn watch that needed repairing and the peace of Jerusalem to God's throne with equal assurance. Papa prayed before every meal and afterwards too, and though his prayers would vary, always there were two things for which he would pray: the Queen and the Second Coming of Jesus Christ.

He did not feel awkward loving his children. Nothing would deter him from his nightly ritual of climbing the narrow spiral stairs to pray with each one of them and tuck them into bed. After the prayer, Papa would lean over his little Corrie and gently put his hand on her face and say, "Sleep well, Corrie . . . I love you."

Corrie remembers, "I would try to remain as still as possible, not wanting to lose the touch of his hand until I went to sleep. Years later in the concentration camp in Germany I would remember the feeling of Father's hand and would pray, 'Oh Lord, let me feel *Your* hand upon me. May I creep under the shadow of *Your* wings.' "

Early in her life Corrie learned of the love and security of her Heavenly Father through the love and gentle example of her Papa.

A lesson Corrie's father taught her often helped in the years that were to come. He would say, "Happiness is not dependent on happenings, but on relationships in the happenings."

With Corrie sitting on his lap, he would tell about his early married life. Although he and his beloved young wife were poor and business was bad, they were happy together—very happy. At first they lived in a little, narrow house in the Jewish section of Amsterdam, and their relationship with their neighbors allowed them to take part in their Sabbaths and in their holy days. Studies of the Old Testament were shared together and sometimes the New Testament. A love for the Jewish people had been kindled in Papa ten Boom's heart by *his* father, so it came naturally to him to mix with and learn more about God's ancient people and their noble culture. As his little family grew, a love for the Jews was instilled in Corrie and her brother and sisters. When Papa inherited the Beje from his father, he continued the tradition there of praying daily for "the peace of Jerusalem."

Mama ten Boom, a woman of striking appearance and an infectious sense of humor, loved to have her home filled with people. The little house was already crowded with four children, three aunts, Papa, and herself, but somehow she always found room for one more person around the oval family dining table. Through this, Corrie learned that hospitality did not depend on how much one had to give materially, but on sharing whatever the Lord had given. The quantity of soup in the pot would be increased by an extra portion of water—but the kindness with which it was served must have made it taste delicious to the guests that came to the Beje—many with such desperate needs.

When guests came, Mama would put a small box on the dining table, saying, "You are welcome in our house, and because we are grateful for your coming, we will add a penny to the blessing box for missionaries."

Whenever Mama heard of a need, she would find time in her busy life to alleviate that one's suffering. Sometimes it would only be through the soup pot or her sewing basket, but people instinctively knew she cared. Birthdays were remembered, notes sent, flowers left after a visit.

How she loved flowers and longed for a yard big enough to grow them and to be able to look up into the sky. Eventually, she made the little flat roof of the Beje her garden, and there she could find moments of beauty and release in her busy, caring life.

When Mama became an invalid because of a stroke, she continued to mold her children's lives. As she sat in her chair by the window, she prayed for her family and all who passed by. All those around her knew she loved them—and loved not only those in the Beje, or Haarlem—but the whole world. Through her example Corrie says, "I learned that love is larger than the walls which shut it in."

For this family an evening of delight would involve a homemade music fest around the piano or a walk to the nearby cathedral, Saint Bavo's. There they would sit in a corridor outside the sanctuary, because they could not pay to hear the concert from within. The cold stones were forgotten as they listened to some great artist interpret Bach on the superb, world-famous pipe organ.

Into the tapestry of Corrie's young life were woven threads of beauty, love, and wisdom. She early recognized Jesus Christ as the Author of it all, and when she was only five, she yielded her life to Him. It was her mother's joy to lead her little daughter to Jesus.

Corrie remembers, "She took my little hand in hers and we prayed together. It was so simple and yet Jesus Christ says that we all must come as children, no matter what our age, social standing, or intellectual background."

Through that experience Corrie began to pray for others. At such an early age, the Lord gave her a heart that was burdened for so many who, in the world's eyes, did not seem worth remembering.

At the back of the Beje was a street called the Smedestraat. It had many bars and saloons, and often while Corrie was playing she would see men come staggering by and fall to the ground. This frightened her, especially when she would watch the police come and haul them off to the police station nearby. She would run to her mother crying, afraid these sick men would be hurt. Always her mother would say, "Pray for them, Corrie," and this is precisely what that little girl did. (One day Corrie and her family would be taken to that same police station for helping the hunted Jews of Holland.)

Years later, Corrie was on a television program in Holland. Afterwards she received a letter which read:

My husband was especially interested because you told us that you had lived in Haarlem. He lived in a house on the Smedestraat. Three years ago he accepted the Lord Jesus as his Savior.

Here was an answer to little Corrie's prayers of so many years before!

This incident reminded Corrie of something that had happened, as she sat around a campfire talking with eighteen young girls. Each one had either lived on the Smedestraat or their parents lived there at some time. They laughed at the coincidence, but Corrie knew it was no coincidence. These girls had been brought together because of their love for Christ, and Corrie told them that years before, as a little child, she had prayed for that street and its occupants. She said to them, "The fact that we have been talking about Jesus, and that God has used me to help reach some of your parents, is an answer to the prayer of a little child. Never doubt whether God hears our prayers, even the unusual ones."

In Haarlem there was a man whom most of the town went out of their way to avoid. They called him *Gekke Thys* (Crazy Thys) and people dismissed him as being an idiot—the town tramp. But Corrie, when only five years old, would pray for him every morning and evening, ". . . and Lord, be with all the people in the Smedestraat and also Gekke Thys."

It was through the plight of this man that a deep concern and love was created in Corrie for the mentally retarded. She touched so many of their lives with her love, and when she was an adult, she started clubs for them, teaching them about a Savior who loved them too.

To this day, nestled in the walls of the great medieval Cathedral of Saint Bavo are low-ceilinged little stores that have been there for generations. One of them is an antique shop run by an elderly, white-haired lady. Amid the warm glow of old copper and brass, exquisite china, and the mellow patina of furniture polished lovingly by many hands over the years, Miss Gert Veldhuisen remembers Corrie as a school friend of hers:

> We attended the School van Loran. Corrie was such a chubby, healthy little girl. . . full of mischief which often got her into trouble. But mostly I remember her as being happy.

Corrie's first day of school was very difficult for her—she behaved as many children do. Protesting, tearful, she had to be almost dragged there. But she soon found out how much she would love her lessons. It was the beginning of a world of learning to read and write—and years later that learning would be used to bring millions comfort and strength through her many writings.

Corrie recalls that she was always dreaming up pranks. "*Mischief was my middle name.*" The schoolmaster, Mr. van Loran, was a strict disciplinarian. One day Corrie had not listened to his instructions, so she felt his hand come crashing across her little face. Humiliated in front of all her friends, she ran home with tears streaming down her cheeks. She had never known such treatment in her home.

Her mother comforted her little "Correman" (a favorite pet name for her). Then Papa ten Boom held Corrie, and she remembers the feeling of safety, as she put her head on his shoulder. One day she was to write of the incident: "What security to have a refuge when life is really hard." (Years later, on the night of her arrest in the Beje, when the Gestapo officer's hand came crashing across her face, she recalled that incident at school, the comfort of her parents, and the refuge that is in Jesus Christ.)

There was no thought of the price of discipleship for Corrie, as she was growing up. Hadn't Papa told her that "God hath not given us the spirit of fear; but of power, and of love, and of a sound mind"(2 Timothy 1:7 KJV) and that Jesus is her hiding place and her shield? Her child's mind could not imagine what there was to fear, or from what she would need to hide. She only knew that Jesus was her friend, and knowing that was enough.

Corrie's first encounter with dying to self became the focal point of her adult commitment to Christ. It came through the door of a broken heart. Sister Nollie married, and Willem too fell in love and left the Beje to establish his own home. Betsie decided she could never marry, because of her faltering health. But Corrie lost her heart at age fourteen to Karel, a handsome ministerial student. The years that brought Corrie to womanhood also matured Karel's interest in her love.

His parents' expectation for him to "marry well" ended the budding courtship. Though Willem warned Corrie of the futility of her dreams with Karel, she refused to believe it, until the day there was that knock at the door.

When Corrie opened it, there stood Karel. "Corrie, I want you to meet my fiancee!" were the words that greeted the brokenhearted young girl. There would be no more walks in the countryside, Karel by her side, and Corrie dreaming of a future together.

Sobbing under the pain, Corrie found comfort in the words of her dear father: "It is love that hurts you, Corrie. It is the strongest force in all the world. When it is blocked, it causes much pain. You can do two things with this love that hurts so much. You can kill it so it will stop hurting, or you can ask your Heavenly Father to change your love into His kind of love. You can ask God to help you love Karel in His way, the better way."

Corrie remembers what she prayed when she went to her bedroom: "Lord, You know that sometime ago I surrendered my life to You. But now I surrender anew, especially that part of my spirit and mind that is wounded by what has happened. You know Lord, that I have a longing to marry. But Jesus, when I give You that part of my body, soul, and mind, I trust that Your victory will be demonstrated exactly there. Take it, Lord. It is Yours."

The battle was strong within her, but then came the victory. It was a victory of trusting. God was asking her to believe that His plan for her life was better . . . fuller . . . than any plan she would ever choose for herself. When she came to the point of trusting Him, she found God's promised peace. She says, "I never brought a child to birth, but I thank the Lord for using me to bring some to rebirth. That is the greatest joy for a Christian. Perhaps this was a bit of losing my life for Jesus and therefore winning it."

The doors to the Beje remained open even after Mama's death and the death of the aunts. Now it was Betsie who set the extra place around the oval table. She took over the homemaking, while Corrie found a place at her father's workbench. Corrie quickly learned watchmaking and, becoming Holland's first licensed female watchmaker, opened the door for other women to enter that field.

When World War I left thousands homeless and orphaned, the oval table saw new faces around it. Little Willie came from the streets of Berlin, a frightened, bedraggled child, whose eyes showed his sadness and bewilderment. He had stood waiting at the railway station, after all the other orphans had been taken to homes. Papa learned that the lady Willie was to live with was ill and could not take him. The ten Booms took the little homeless boy into the warmth of the Beje, along with another orphan already assigned there.

Twenty-eight years later, Corrie was in West Berlin, speaking at a meeting. Afterwards she saw a well-dressed man waiting to talk with her. His smile seemed to be familiar. "Tante Corrie, do you remember me? I'm Willie, who lived with your family many years ago."

This man—so different from that bewildered child, and with a light that shone in his eyes—told her of the deep effect living at the Beje had upon him. He had never before heard people pray in their homes, but for the ten Booms it was a completely natural way of life. Years later, he accepted Jesus Christ because of the seeds of His love that Tante Corrie and her family had planted in the heart of that frightened, little boy, who needed love so desperately.

When Corrie heard of a lonely woman, friendless in a mental hospital, she became her friend, even though it was a four-hour trip to visit her. Love was worth the effort in Corrie's life. Often Corrie has said, "Whenever you come in contact with feebleminded people, please, please tell them that Jesus loves them. They often understand God's love better than other people who have problems understanding it, because of their intellectual doubt. Paul wrote in First Corinthians 1:20, 21, 'For consider what have the philosopher, the writer and the critic of this world to show for all their wisdom? Has not God made the wisdom of this world look foolish? For it was after the world in its wisdom had failed to know God, that he in his wisdom chose to save all who would believe by the "simple-mindedness" of the gospel message.' " (PHILLIPS).

About her work with the mentally retarded, Papa said, "Corrie, what you do among these people is of little importance in the eyes of men, but I'm sure in God's eyes it is the most valuable work of all."

Corrie's most extensive ministry outside the home was her work in girls' clubs. She founded the Triangle Clubs of Haarlem, seeking to provide opportunities for recreation and spiritual training for girls between the ages of twelve and eighteen. (Later the age limit would be put aside, as Corrie could not bear to stop *anyone* from coming!)

In a bright, cheerful apartment house for the elderly in The Hague, an even brighter, cheerful seventy-nine-year-old lady recalls her times with Corrie in the Triangle Clubs. Paula Monsanto's big, brown, mischievous eyes dance with delight as she talks of Corrie, her friend with the twinkling blue eyes.

As a young girl I remember going to the clubs shortly after I became a Christian. Oh, what happy times they were for me. What a leader Corrie was! Always ready to help people. All her family was like that, especially good old Papa.

Paula's eyes clouded for a minute, as she remembered this beloved old man.

Corrie was so wonderful with the children and especially the mentally retarded—she gave so much of herself. Their eyes would light up when they saw her. Oh, Corrie . . . how much I love her!

(During the war years, Paula would once again have the experience of the ten Boom's love reaching out to her, as she and her sister Meta would be hidden from the Nazis in the Beje.)

In the twenty-five years that Corrie worked with the club girls, she stood by many of their deathbeds. Time after time she was able to place the dying hand of one of "her girls" into the hand of Jesus Christ. (Scores of women living in Holland—and some around the world—remember with joy those "club days," when Corrie challenged them to give their lives to Christ and to appreciate the Bible as the Living Word of God.)

Already Papa's prayer that his child would bear fruit for the Lord was being answered, but the years ahead would reveal an even greater harvest. Before this would take place, however, Corrie would go through what perhaps could be some of the most evil experiences that man will ever perpetrate on another human being.

". . . except a [grain] of wheat fall into the ground and die, it abideth alone: but if it die, it bringeth forth much fruit."

John 12:24

Mama and Papa ten Boom.

Mama with Willem and Betsie.

Corrie, when she was three,
with Nollie (1895).

Betsie, Willem, Nollie with Corrie
(at the age when she came to the Lord).

The School van Loran. Corrie is in the third row, fourth from right.
Mr. van Loran is seated on the right.

Corrie and Nollie dressed
in their Sunday best.

The Grote Markt, 1898.
The Barteljorisstraat is on the left,
with flags flying.

The Barteljorisstraat, 1935, with the ten Boom
watch shop on the right, at the rear of the tram.

Nollie, Corrie, Willem, and Betsie
pose for a formal portrait in 1910.

Nollie, Betsie, and Corrie.

Nollie and Betsie read in the living
room of the Beje, while a friend
(center) enjoys the stereopticon.

A lovely photo of Betsie.

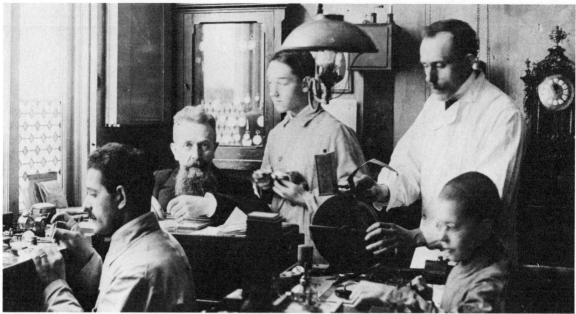
Papa and his assistants in the watch shop.

The three sisters (Nollie, Corrie, Betsie) with Mama, Papa, Willem, and two aunts.

Nollie's wedding.

Papa, surrounded by the family, holds his first grandson, Casper.

Papa's delight—his grandchildren.

Papa with his children and grandchildren and the family kitten.

Corrie, with shovel, camps out with her club girls.

Corrie looks out of carriage window, while Papa and the club girls await the start of a parade.

Corrie, the drummer (left) about to lead the club girls in a march!

Betsie, Puck (raised as a foster child), Papa, and Corrie.

A born leader, Corrie holds the attention of the girls.

Bewildered bus driver about to drive Corrie and her girls back to Haarlem.

This scene from the film THE HIDING PLACE depicts Corrie with her very special love–retarded children.

Holland's first woman watchmaker—
Corrie, as played by Jeannette Clift.

Corrie, Betsie, and Papa enjoy
a ride along a canal.

Papa and Betsie walking together.

Papa and Betsie (on left) while
on holiday in Germany.

2

Clouds of War

The Nazis occupy Haarlem.

The ten Booms celebrated the one-hundredth anniversary of their watch shop in January of 1937. In a way it also marked the end of their peaceful way of life. The world around them was changing. The changes would demand a response from this God-fearing family.

The radio, a prize possession given to Papa by his friends during a serious illness, broadened their horizons. How wonderful to be able to hear news from abroad! Nightly they listened together with such interest, as the programs brought them in close contact with the world.

But some of the news was distressing. A man with a demonic force (named Adolf Hitler) was gaining tremendous power, as he and his hordes declared war on the little countries around them. The Dutch Prime Minister assured the nation that Holland would remain neutral—

there was no need for alarm. Five hours later, Germany attacked Holland, and with little resistance, took over the country.

The ten Booms sat in shock, hardly believing their ears, as the announcement came over the radio. Almost in disbelief, they went about their daily tasks, until they heard the announcement that the Queen had left Holland. The crackling of the radio, as a BBC announcer from London introduced Her Majesty, Queen Wilhelmina, whose words jolted them into reality:

> Fellow Hollanders, the lights have gone out over free Holland. Where only two weeks ago there was a free nation of men and women with a cherished tradition of Christian civilization, there is now the stillness of death. Oppressed, threatened, watched on every side by a power that would tear out all hope from the soul of man, the unhappy people of Holland can only pray in silence.
>
> For those that have lost their voice, but not their hope, or their vision in the struggle against the onslaught of barbarianism . . . long live the Netherlands!

The ten Booms, great lovers of the royal family and their beloved native land, wept openly.

At first there seemed to be little change in the country, except for the sight of German soldiers everywhere. The sound of tanks and the goose-stepping soldiers on the cobblestone street echoed through the little rooms of the Beje. Betsie would encounter the Germans on her daily excursions to buy food at the Grote Markt. It was strange to hear German being spoken everywhere.

Then came food rationing and the radio spouting propaganda instead of news. Most disturbing of all was the beginning of the harassment of the Jewish neighbors—at first in notices put up everywhere: JEWS FORBIDDEN; next their shops were being closed, and then orders that every Jew had to wear a yellow star. (Because of his great love for this people, Papa insisted on standing openly in line to get a star, too.)

When Papa and Corrie were out walking near the fish market one day, they saw men, women, and children being herded into a truck. All were wearing the yellow star. Their destination would be Germany and the bestial concentration camps. To a horrified Corrie, Papa said sadly, "I pity the poor Germans, Corrie. They have touched the apple of God's eye!"

As Corrie watched, she knew what she had to do. "Lord Jesus, I offer myself for Your people . . . in any way, any place, any time."

As she prayed she began to understand a dream she had had months before. In the dream she was in the Grote Markt. She saw herself, Betsie, Papa, and others she knew being herded into an old farm wagon and taken away against their will.

It was not long before the ten Boom's house became a sanctuary for the Jews, hiding from their sadistic hunters. The little Beje was bursting at the seams, as it became one of the underground headquarters.

Corrie, now in charge of eighty people (called the "Beje gang"), could turn no one away. She arranged for hundreds of frightened Jewish people to find a haven in other houses in the country.

Corrie's brother, Willem, now a minister, was being watched by the police, as he became more and more involved in the work. He told Corrie not to come to him for assistance anymore for her own safety, so she joined forces with the national Dutch underground leaders.

Space was an important problem in the Beje. An area in which to hide had to be found, and it was decided Corrie's bedroom was the place in which to build a secret room. In a space only thirty inches deep, at the back of Corrie's bed, a false wall was cleverly built, leaving space for people to hide. On their hands and knees, Betsie and Corrie crawled into that room and prayed it might protect their precious charges, if ever needed. An underground member came to inspect it and, striking the false wall, said, "The Gestapo could search for a year, but they'll never find this one!"

A warning buzzer was installed, and Corrie remembers: "We practiced safety drills often. After everyone had gone to bed, I would press one of the alarm bells. Our guests would disappear into the hiding place. If they did it quickly, I would reward them by treating them to cream puffs. They'd often say, 'Aren't we going to have an alarm tonight? We're hungry for cream puffs.' " Food was an ever-increasing problem, since the Jews were not issued ration cards. Through the underground, Corrie managed to obtain one hundred cards, so her flock did not go hungry.

Corrie would admonish her underground workers not to take risks, but she herself would often forget her own words of caution! To the amusement of the local baker, she would buy ten large loaves of bread. Shaking his head, as he watched her go down the street, often passing German soldiers with her unusually cumbersome load, the baker would say, "So much bread for one old man and two middle-aged ladies. They must have many birds to feed!"

Corrie speaks of those days as being happy ones in spite of the fear in which they all had to live. "The Beje had the reputation of being the happiest house in the underground. I don't think I ever laughed as much as when we were hiding the Jews in our house. I myself enjoy so very much the Jewish sense of humor!"

A message was passed on to Corrie one day that a Jewish orphanage in Amsterdam was going to be raided. All the babies were to be killed. Immediately she contacted the thirty teenage boys who worked with her in the underground and asked them to help. *Save the babies of the Jewish orphanage*, were her orders. She did not want to know the details of exactly how they would do it, because later, if caught, she would be tortured until she told how it had been accomplished. Corrie did know that her workers had used German uniforms taken from soldiers who had defected.

"Sometimes German civilians and soldiers would come to us and say, 'We will not go on working for Adolf Hitler. He is no good. Can you help us?' I would hide these soldiers on a farm for the duration of the war. When they were hidden, I would take their uniforms and my boys, my underground workers, would often accomplish deeds attired in the uniform of their enemy. Later I learned that the boys, dressed in the uniforms, drew up to the orphanage in trucks and demanded the little babies. The orphanage workers believed they were Nazis and wept as they handed over their little charges. Little did they know then that they were to be saved, for the boys then drove to the outskirts of the city and, helped by my teenage underground girls, were able to distribute them into many different homes. I would hold a baby in my hands and say, 'Will you save this baby? If you don't, it will be killed!' Of course they took the baby. It was a joy to see all of them saved."

Some years after the war, Corrie was speaking at a church in Australia when she met a Dutchman who said to her, "Do you remember that I once lived in Haarlem, your hometown? And do you remember that you brought me a Jewish baby of two weeks old?"

Corrie replied that she could not remember specifically, because there were about a hundred babies to be saved that night, and just where each one was placed would be difficult for her to recall.

The Dutchman went on: "I will never forget it! We had a baby that had died and my wife cried constantly. She would go to the child's room, and look at the little crib, and all the clothes she had prepared for him. 'I have everything for the baby in my heart, but my hands are empty!' Then there was a knock at the door and standing there was a young boy who said, 'Corrie ten Boom asked if you would save a Jewish baby?' Of course we said 'yes.' We adopted him after the war. Later we came here to Australia, and he has always been a good son to us."

The man turned from Corrie and, with a voice that was choked with emotion, called to a boy standing near. A handsome, tall fourteen-year-old Jewish boy walked up to Corrie. The proud father said, "Corrie, this is the baby boy you brought to us that day . . . Martin, this is the lady who saved your life!"

Corrie was so deeply moved to see this beautiful child. As she hugged him, she could not help but think of all the other children who must be alive somewhere in the world at that moment because of her work with those faithful underground workers. She was so thankful to the Lord.

Martin and Corrie became friends, and he asked her many questions. Over a Dutch cup of coffee at his home, he just kept looking at her: *the lady who saved my life!* The next day Martin went to school and asked his teacher if he could say something to the students. When given permission, Martin stood before the whole class and proudly told of the fearless Dutch lady he had met the day before. She had saved his life when he was only two weeks old. Very simply, he quietly told his fellow students, "I believe that I will be a good boy all the time now, for she has also taught me how to ask Jesus to come into my heart."

This was evidence to Corrie that Martin had really experienced Jesus in his young life. For she believes, "When Jesus is in your heart, you have a burden to share it with others."

One of the Dutch boys who helped rescue those Jewish babies from the orphanage that night said to Corrie that he believed the most important work they could do was that of saving lives. The name of the boy was Pete den Hartog, and Corrie said to him, "Pete, I think we do important work when I think of the babies we have saved, but there is a work that is more important, and that is saving souls by telling people about Jesus."

Pete looked at her for a moment and then laughed. He said, "I am a Christian. I read my Bible. I pray. I go to church. But telling people about Jesus—that is the business of my pastor."

Quietly Corrie put her hand on his shoulder and said, "Pete, *every* Christian is called to be a soul winner for Jesus. He has said, 'as the Father has sent me, so I send you.' And in your life there will come a time when you will see *that* as the most important work for you."

Six months later Pete was arrested and was told that he had only one week to live. The day before he was killed, he wrote the ten Booms a letter:

> All the boys in my cell are sentenced to death. I am so glad that I could tell them about Jesus and they have accepted Him. I know that when they shoot us tomorrow, we will *all* go to heaven, because we have brought our sins to Jesus and He has made us all children of God. We know that the house of the Father with many mansions is our very close future. I see now that the most important work for a Christian *is* to win souls for eternity.

Corrie was so thankful to receive that letter. She knew that whatever the Germans would do to their bodies, because of Pete's witness in prison each one of those men would be with Christ.

. . . he that winneth souls is wise.
                                          Proverbs 11:30 KJV

Casper ten Boom, Corrie's papa, on the 100th anniversary of the watch shop, 1937.

The Germans enter Haarlem, 1940.

German artillery in the streets.

Papa (played by Arthur O'Connell in THE HIDING PLACE) wears the Jewish star.

Betsie (played by Julie Harris in THE HIDING PLACE) passes German soldiers in the Grote Markt.

Collecting radios from the Dutch (from the film THE HIDING PLACE).

Actual photograph of children being evacuated from Haarlem.

The Beje quickly filled up with Jews who needed hiding (from the film THE HIDING PLACE).

3

A Refuge

Refugees at the Beje.

Constantly Corrie was faced with dozens of requests for help. She knew her organization was too big for her to handle, yet she knew she could not stop, even though the price of a mistake was deadly high. Corrie often wondered, *How long?*

Bach's music was a soothing balm in those dark moments. When Corrie's heart ached under all the oppressive ugliness of the occupation, she would sit at the piano and play the familiar music of her favorite composer. Then, too, Nollie's son, Peter van Woerden, who was an accomplished pianist, would visit the Beje and play for its inhabitants.

Peter, now an evangelist in Switzerland, talked of his experiences with his Tante Corrie in those days:

36

At sixteen I was too young to realize all that was going on. I once played the National Anthem on the organ in church, for which I was arrested and thrown into prison. But it was worth it, because I came to know the Lord there!

Because young boys were constantly sent off to Germany, Tante Corrie and Tante Betsie would dress me up as a girl, so I could go out on the street. I even got whistled at by the German soldiers! But Tante Corrie was reluctant to let me help in the underground work, because she always said I got into enough trouble doing nothing!

The Beje now had seven *permanent* guests: Jews who were too obviously Jewish to run the gauntlet of escape, as well as young Dutch men, some of them active in the underground. Hans Poley was one of these young men.

Today Hans works as an Environmental Advisor for the Shell Companies in Holland. He was only nineteen when the ten Boom family hid him in their home. That was in May 1943. Corrie was a friend of Hans's mother, and she knew the Nazis were sending all young men his age to Germany to work in the munitions factories. Each day Hans expected to be herded on to a cattle train and taken hundreds of miles from his homeland. When he moved into the Beje, the underground managed to get him false papers which described him as an "evangelist." (At this point in the war the Germans still tolerated ministers.)

Recently Hans and his wife, Mies, dining in a restaurant overlooking the Grote Market in Haarlem, recalled the days at the Beje with a sense of thankfulness, despite the horror.

The Beje was very crowded. Four people sleeping in one small room. Then it seemed ample, but now—now I wonder how we made it. Each day there were twelve to fifteen people to cook meals for. I helped to prepare the meals, peeling potatoes, doing dishes, and so forth. Then there was general housework that everyone took part in. Fresh air could only be had by going up on the small flat roof of the Beje.

It was not surprising to Hans that Corrie became involved in the underground.

With such vitality and drive and concern, she just had to do something!

He remembers her taking great risks to help people, always praying and trusting the Lord to lead her. She would even have to ask the Lord to help her remember where she had carelessly placed important little pieces of paper with top-secret messages on them. Hans continued relating his thoughts of life with the ten Booms:

> The days and nights would have been unbearable but for the hope that kept alive. Papa ten Boom brought to us such hope. He would lead us in a prayer meeting each evening and would take everything to the Lord that concerned each one of us. Our families, our friends—some who had already been arrested—everything was given over to the Lord. Papa ten Boom was an island of rest in a buzzing beehive. His was an unshakable faith in the Lord.
>
> Tante Betsie quietly went about the household, organizing everything, and welcoming anyone who came to the door. Her health was not good, and because of the tremendous strain, she was often ill.

Besides playing many games in the Beje to pass the time, lessons were taught to one another at night. The Jews would teach Hebrew, others would teach Italian—or even cooking (though there was little food), and first aid. Hans taught astronomy and, of course, Papa taught the Bible.

Even in those dark days, Cupid was working in the Beje—Cupid in the form of an undaunted Dutch lady named Corrie.

When Hans came to live at the Beje, he was very much in love with seventeen-year-old Mies Wessels, who lived in Zeeland, not too far from Haarlem. Both of their families agreed it was much too dangerous for them to meet together, so they did not see each other for the first eight months Hans lived with the ten Booms. Corrie knew how much young Hans missed his beautiful Mies, with her blond hair and blue eyes—the perfect picture one envisions a Dutch girl to be. Corrie's special gift to Hans for Christmas 1943 was to allow Mies to spend Christmas Day in the Beje.

How excited they both were at the prospect of seeing each other, even if only for a few hours. Hans recalls:

The boys found or made little gifts for the ladies in the Beje, not knowing that the ladies were making gifts for them. That way we had a little bit of Santa Claus!

That Christmas was celebrated side by side with Hanukkah. Betsie found an old Hanukkah menorah and put it on the piano. The light from the candles flickered across their faces: Papa, Betsie, Corrie, Eusie, Mary, Thea, Leendert, Meta Monsanto, Henk, and Hans and the specially invited guest, Mies.

It was not a Christmas dinner of turkey and all the trimmings. To the beleagured Dutch, whatever was edible that could be put on the table for Christmas dinner was cause enough to thank the Lord. (It would not be long before tulip bulbs would be devoured, as food was becoming more and more scarce.)

For dinner that Christmas, Mies only remembers "some kind of salad, made into pyramids" but the food was of secondary importance. Just to be with Hans transcended any meal.

The memory of those brief hours would have to satisfy this young couple for many months. Each day Mies lived in dread of Hans being arrested, as she knew he was involved in so many underground activities.

Late one night Corrie learned that a man for whom the Germans had been looking was to be arrested the next day. Hastily she climbed the narrow stairs and as quietly as possible awakened the sleeping Hans. Whispering, so as not to awaken the others, she asked Hans to go and warn the man. He immediately dressed. Opening the side door of the Beje, he looked into the dark alley to be certain he was not being watched. Quickly he made his way through the deserted streets to the railway station. At five o'clock in the morning he was on his way to Soest, the town where the man lived. As he sat in the train, his eyes heavy with sleep, he was unaware of the identity of several nearby passengers.

Alighting at Soest, he quickly hurried to the address given to him by Corrie. The door was opened, and Hans slipped in to warn of the impending arrest. As he was leaving, relieved that he had been able to accomplish his task, the Gestapo (who had been on the same train) were waiting outside the door. Hans and the man were arrested. Hans today tells the story quietly:

> The Nazis never found out the ten Booms had any involvement. Several weeks before, the Gestapo had attempted to arrest a young Dutchman whom I knew. When trying to escape, he had been killed when jumping to his death out of a window. The Lord made them believe my story that that man had been my contact.

News of Hans's arrest traveled quickly through the underground. Mies remembers coming home that night.

> I was expecting a happy celebration, as it was my father's birthday. Everyone seemed to be acting so strangely. After dinner they broke the news to me. I shall never forget the shock. Hans was in an Amsterdam prison. I was now eighteen years old and deeply in love. I was desolate.

Hans remained in that prison for six weeks and then was sent to Amersfoort concentration camp, one-and-a-half hours from Haarlem.

Shortly after his transportation to Amersfoort, a letter came to Mies. The envelope was written in a hand that was foreign to her. Upon opening it, she found inside a letter written to her by Hans—every part of the piece of paper written on in tiny, precise writing.

In being transported, Hans had thrown the letter out of the train, hoping someone would find it and mail it to Mies. His hopes were realized. They are so thankful that the Lord led a fellow Dutchman, not known to them, to find that precious communication. Every day that followed, Mies wondered if Hans had been shot. This went on for over eight months. That letter was read over and over again to comfort her. She says:

> I still have it. It is worn by being read so many times, but it is very precious to me.

Hans meanwhile was trying to adjust to prison life.

> It was hard, but I just threw everything on the Lord. I just trusted Him. His promises brought me comfort, and I would remember

psalms and hymns I had sung as a child in our church and in the Beje.

In 1949 Hans and Mies were married, and their love story, kept alive by Corrie even in the midst of war, continues today.

Paula Monsanto, who now lives in The Hague, remembers with gratitude when she and her sister Meta went to stay at the Beje. They had been brought up as Lutherans, even though their grandfather was Jewish.

> During the early part of the war I worked as a nurse. At the hospital I had to fill in some papers. One question asked whether I was a Christian or Jewish. Knowing I was partly Jewish I wrote down that I *was* a Jew—being a Christian I did not want to lie!
>
> When we Jews had to register, the Nazis sent me to the *schul* to get the yellow star to wear everywhere. When I knocked on the door, I asked for Mr. Schul! What an uninformed Jew I was—I did not even realize that *schul* meant "synagogue"!

One day, two Dutch policemen came to the Monsanto home and told them they must leave. The police had orders to pick them up that evening. Paula remembered that Corrie had said that, if ever the police came, they were to go to the Beje. Quickly Paula and Meta took a few things and went to hide in the ten Boom house.

> We were all supposed to help with the housework. Meta helped peel potatoes, but I was never very good at that sort of thing. I made good conversation! . . . But Papa, ah, he was the one who made good conversation to the Lord! Once one of the young, underground boys needed money for the transportation of some Jews to a safe place. Corrie gave him all the money she had, which was just the right amount. Then Papa heard there was no more money in the house for food, so he said, "We will ask the Lord." About an hour after he finished praying, the doorbell rang, and there was a lady with one thousand guilders!
>
> But Corrie is like that too; she speaks to God about everything . . . and He answers! I am jealous of her! She lives so closely to Him!

One evening an old Jewish man and his family came for refuge to the ten Booms. There was not enough room for everyone, so Corrie asked Paula if she would stay with Hans Poley's parents, just fifty minutes away. Paula left that night, saying good-bye to the ten Booms and her sister—not knowing if she would ever see them again. Paula continued, as she reminisced about those days, with tears of gratitude in her eyes:

> I pray for Corrie every day . . . It is my way of saying, "Thank you"—not just for me and Meta, but for all the Jews.
> I will never forget dear Corrie!

Another guest who became one of the more permanent ones was Meyer Mossel, a Jewish cantor from Amsterdam. Hans Poley brought him to the Beje after the cantor's wife and child had fled from their home in hopes of finding sanctuary. Each day he lived with the fear that his little family had been found and arrested. The ten Booms loved this proud leader of their Jewish friends, calling him "Eusie." His humor and stories made many of the agonizing days brighter. His magnificent voice filled the house, and often he had to be warned not to sing so loudly—it could be heard in the street!

Sometimes there would be arguments when Eusie would refuse to do his share of the household chores. He felt he was entitled to a five-day workweek. Saturday was his Sabbath, and out of respect for the Christians, he would observe Sunday as theirs. He could not possibly work on those two days!

Once he got a lecture from Corrie. Shortly before he died in 1978, he recalled the incident.

> One day I remember we had been complaining about our living conditions and Tante Corrie heard about it. Sitting by the stove and waving a big poker, she gave us a very strict sermon. I had never seen her angry before, but she was right. It was not long before she was laughing with us again, however!
> We lived under such tension that sometimes we laughed so much. Some little thing would set us off . . . it was just a way of release.

Papa loved to talk to Eusie about the Old Testament. The two of them often spent many happy hours together discussing it.

On February 28, 1944, Corrie awakened with a sick, sinking feeling. The fever she had had for two days was not abating. Betsie stood at the end of her bed with a cup of herb tea, hoping to remedy, in some small way, her sister's attack of the flu. As Corrie sipped her tea, Betsie told her a man was waiting downstairs and would see no one else but her.

Painfully Corrie dressed and struggled down the narrow, winding stairs, so ill that everything seemed unreal to her. As she entered the little shop, the man standing nervously before her seemed as if he were part of a nightmare. As he introduced himself as Jan Vogel, his eyes shifted furtively about the room. He spoke quickly, telling that his wife had just been arrested for helping Jews. Soon he feared the Gestapo would be questioning her. For six hundred guilders he could get her released and save many in the underground.

Corrie felt there was something strange about this man who would not look her in the eye. But her fever impaired her judgment, and she promised she would get the money for him.

She gave instructions for the money to be obtained from the bank and the amount handed to this supposedly distraught man. Climbing the stairs with difficulty, Corrie returned to her bed and gratefully sank into a deep, feverish sleep—a sleep that was later interrupted by the sound of a buzzer, and people running past her bed, into the hiding place. Then Corrie realized this was no mere rehearsal, this was the real thing. The Gestapo were in the Beje!

The man with the guilty eyes—a modern-day Judas—had betrayed them. A fellow Dutchman had sold this family and so many of their friends for a meager six hundred guilders.

The Germans hunted through the house for the hiding place, but they never found it. The ten Booms had called it the "angel crib," believing guardian angels would watch over its precious contents.

Eusie recalled:

> When the alarm buzzer sounded, we ran into Tante Corrie's room—into the secret hiding place. There, six of us crowded into its small area. It is impossible to describe. Not daring to make a

sound—not a cough or a sneeze. Toilet conditions were much like Tante Corrie must have experienced in Ravensbruck . . . The air was claustrophobic. When we were finally rescued from the hiding place two days later by underground workers, I prayed: "Thank You, O Lord Eternal, who has brought us through this and kept us alive and who has given us life to this moment!"

It was not the end of staying underground for me, of course. In thanking Tante Corrie and her family, I want to say that there were a few more Dutch houses that would take Jews in, but not very many.

(Eusie, who became a rabbi, was never caught by the Germans. After the war, he was reunited with his wife and child.)

All of Papa's family were in the house the night it was raided. All were arrested. Betsie and Corrie, their faces swollen and bloody from the beating the Gestapo had given them, helped their dear father as they were led away from the home they had known for so many years. Papa stopped only to wind one of the clocks as he passed by.

Exactly one hundred years before, Corrie's grandfather, in that same house, had offered prayers for the peace of Jerusalem. Now all the ten Booms were being arrested for helping its people.

The people of Haarlem wept as they saw their "Grand Old Man" and his family being taken away by the ruthless Gestapo. Darkness fell over the Barteljorisstraat that day. The Beje would never be the same— no more would Papa's voice be heard there reading the Bible and praying to his Lord. But what had emanated from that little Dutch house would never be silenced.

The ten Boom family had no hiding place that day, none that had been built by man. But as Papa had taught them in the years past, "The Lord is your hiding place." These were to prove to be no mere words . . . .

Hans Poley and Mies Wessels during the war.

Hans and Mies reunited after his release from the concentration camp.

The kitchen of the Beje was a busy place. Here Tante Betsie, left, supervises "Eusie" (in glasses), 1943.

In the living room of the Beje. Seated: Eusie, Mary, Tante Betsie. Standing: Hans and Mr. Verdonck.

Getting fresh air on the Beje roof. Left to right: **Harry, Thea, Hans, Mary, and Eusie.**

Peeling potatoes on the roof. Left to right: **Leendert, Henk, Hans, and Eusie.**

Mary and Thea leave the hiding place after a false alarm.

Corrie helps Betsie, as they are transported after the arrest at the Beje (from the film THE HIDING PLACE).

4

The Family Divided

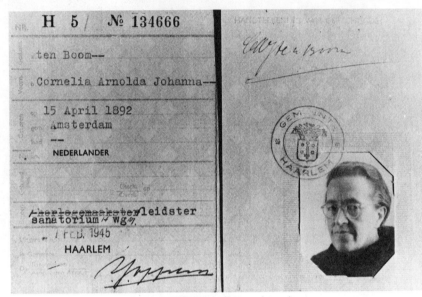

Corrie's official police registration.

The first night of their arrest, the ten Booms were taken to the police station near the Beje. For more than fifty years they had been treated with respect and love by their fellow citizens. Now the ten Booms, in complete contrast, experienced the utmost degradation. But even in jail, their lives would touch others.

Several years after the war, Corrie was in her hometown of Haarlem when she had an accident. It was not serious, but not being able to walk, she needed help from a passing policeman. He then got out his notebook to make a report, and he asked Corrie her name.

"Corrie ten Boom," she replied. Startled, the policeman looked at her and said, "ten Boom? Are you a member of the family arrested ten years ago?" This Dutch policeman had been in the police station the night the Nazis brought in Corrie and her father, together with Betsie, Nollie, Willem, her nephew Peter, and fifty of their friends. There were no beds for them, or even chairs, so they all had to sit on the floor.

The policeman said to Corrie, "I shall never forget that night. There was an atmosphere as if there were a feast, even though most of you were on your way to die in prison. I remember that just before your father tried to sleep, he said, 'Children, let us pray together.' Tired from the ordeal, but with a radiance on his face, he offered comfort from God's Word, Psalms 91:1 [KJV]: *He that dwelleth in the secret place of the most High shall abide under the shadow of the Almighty.*"

In recalling this scene, Corrie likes to think of the day when, in heaven, she would see her father again. Perhaps the conversation would go something like this:

CORRIE: Papa, do you remember that last night in Haarlem in the police station?
PAPA: Yes, Corrie, I remember.
CORRIE: Do you recall the policeman that was on duty?
PAPA: No, I don't seem to remember him, Corrie.

Then with joy, Corrie will be able to tell him the story of that policeman who, unbeknown to Papa, was being touched by the witness of Christian joy and victory that night.

Corrie says of her father: "You know, he did not consciously think that evening, 'I must say something to be a blessing for that policeman.' No, Father lived a very relaxed life, but his whole life was turned toward his Savior. Jesus made Papa a mirror of His joy, so that the policeman— even after ten years—remembered exactly which Psalm Papa had read."

The same unconscious, unrehearsed spirit of love and concern, passed down from Papa, radiates from Corrie. Her life, too, is always turned toward Jesus.

At noon the next day, the family was taken out of Haarlem. As Corrie, still sick, sat huddled with Papa and Betsie, she looked longingly out of the window of the old bus. All the old, familiar scenes so taken for granted—so interwoven into her very life—passed by. Memories welled up, not to be put aside: the cobblestone streets where she had played with Betsie and Nollie; the cathedral with its stone set like a magnificent mosaic—the spire bursting with praise to the Lord. How many times the family had worshiped there and listened to the concerts on the organ. She could hear the bells that had awakened her each day, by which Papa set his clocks. Their melody seemed to be saying a sad farewell.

As they crossed the Grote Markt, Corrie remembered the dream she had had: all of them being taken away across this square, not being able to return. Shuddering, she knew that nothing would ever be the same again. Her family would never be together like this. She held tightly to Papa's and Betsie's hands—Betsie's gentle hands, roughened by the heavy housework—Papa's so frail, showing all of his eighty-four years. How many times those hands had comforted her!

On their arrival at Scheveningen, a large, stark prison on the outskirts of The Hague, they were all separated. The women were taken to their cells first. It happened so quickly, there was no time for lengthy farewells. As Corrie passed Papa, she managed to stop and kiss his noble forehead for the last time: "Father," she cried, "God be with you!"

"And with you, my daughters!" he returned in simple benediction.

This gentle, beloved man's voice was full of love and hope. The sound of it would ring in the sisters' ears in the days ahead, giving them comfort.

From sharing a small cell with five other women, Corrie found herself thrown into solitary confinement. The doctor feared her illness would develop into tuberculosis and infect the other prisoners. Corrie, who had loved the laughter, the everyday noises of living with so many people in the Beje, now was alone—horribly alone—in a cell only two paces wide and six paces long. High up in the filthy wall was a small window, where she could just see the sky and an occasional bird flying by—a contrast of freedom.

Her only possessions were a cup and spoon. The bag she had packed, in case she was ever taken to prison, had been left in front of the door to the hiding place in her bedroom. At the moment of her arrest, she had turned to pick it up. "A short battle in my heart ended with victory, and I was able to choose the safety for the hidden people rather than my own well-being.

"I often summed up what treasures were in that bag: a toothbrush, handkerchief, comb, and so forth. I could have used them so much. But then I thanked the Lord that He had given me the strength to say *no* to the temptation of selfishness.

"Perhaps that bag is the greatest sacrifice I ever made in my life!"

Now in the bleak, dank, evil-smelling cell, the Gospel of John, smuggled to her by a nurse, brought her hope amid the horrifying silence and loneliness. She read and reread old familiar passages, grappling with God's promises:

> I will not leave you comfortless . . . .
>
> John 14:18 KJV

Hitler's birthday gave the guards an excuse to have a party. The prisoners were able to shout information back and forth. Nollie and Willem had been released. All those arrested in that raid on the Beje in February were free, except Betsie and Corrie. Of Papa, Corrie could learn nothing. Months after his death, she received a letter from Nollie, telling her Papa had died in a hospital corridor. Corrie's anguish was beyond measure, until she remembered his most earnest prayer the day that he had held a Jewish baby in his arms. Lovingly he had said: "It would be an honor to give my life for God's ancient people, the Jews."

Corrie spoke softly, in the loneliness of her dark cell, "Yes, Papa, you have seen your honor come, and from the very hands of Jesus! To think you see Him face-to-face . . . and Mama too!"

Papa was no longer imprisoned, at the mercy of cruel guards, but free with his Savior, whom he had loved and served all his life! Papa's favorite saying was: *The best is yet to be!* He had now found the very best, and Corrie knew he would be waiting for that day when they would all be reunited.

> Eye hath not seen, nor ear heard, neither have entered into the heart of man, the things which God hath prepared for them that love him.
>
> 1 Corinthians 2:9 KJV

Corrie had made a small knife out of a bone, and had managed to scratch on her cell wall behind her bed the dates which were so significant to her those past few months.

February 28, 1944	ARREST
February 29, 1944	TRANSPORT TO SCHEVENINGEN
March 16, 1944	BEGINNING OF SOLITARY
April 15, 1944	MY BIRTHDAY IN PRISON

Now she scratched another date:

| *March 10, 1944* | FATHER RELEASED |
| | NOT LOST, BUT GONE BEFORE |

News also came to Corrie that the Jews had escaped safely from the hiding place. Each was relocated and was still safe—all except old Mary Itallie. She was seen later by some German soldiers and was quickly recognized as a Jew and arrested. She disappeared across the borders of Germany.

Germany—the very word was like a threat. The death camps were in Germany—the stench of the incinerators—the ditches filled with corpses. Whispers came back across the borders, and the messages wrapped a pall around the world.

> ". . . and ye shall be brought before rulers and kings for my sake. . . . But when they shall lead you, and deliver you up, take no thought beforehand what ye shall speak, neither do ye premeditate: but whatsoever shall be given you in that hour, that speak ye: for it is not ye that speak, but the Holy [Spirit]."
>
> Mark 13:9, 11 KJV

During that time in solitary confinement, Corrie was brought before the *Sachbearbeiter* (the judge). God used this time to touch the German officer's life.

Hans Rahms, dressed in his lieutenant's uniform, looked as unapproachable as the rest, yet deep in his heart was a longing to be free! After the questioning had been going on for some time, Corrie felt led to say, "You have asked me so many questions, may I ask you one?" He looked at her impassively and said, "Go ahead."

Corrie stood before him as a prisoner, liable to receive the death sentence from this man, yet she sensed that she, because of Christ, was far more free than her captor.

"Is there darkness in your life?"

The officer looked at her for a moment, then replied, "Darkness? There is no light in my life."

Then Corrie told him that Jesus was the light of the world and that everyone who believes in Him does not remain in darkness. The Holy Spirit gave her freedom that day to tell this man of the Savior who had died for him. The officer's face remained stoic, yet Corrie knew her words had had an effect.

Later there came a terrible moment during her questioning when Lieutenant Rahms took out a folder and confronted Corrie with names, addresses, and information that could lead many of her co-workers to death. These had been found in the Beje, together with forbidden photos of the royal family.

Holding them in his hands, he paused for a moment. Then, turning toward the stove, he opened the small door and threw the incriminating evidence into the flames. The Lord had touched his heart. In the "wilderness" experience of Scheveningen prison, God had shown Corrie He still cared. In her heart she praised Him for His goodness. She understood that day, as she watched the flames curl around those papers, what Paul meant in Colossians 2:14 (KJV):

> Blotting out the handwriting of ordinances that was
> against us, which was contrary to us, and took it out
> of the way, nailing it to his cross.

Later Betsie was questioned by this same officer and at the end of each session, prayed with him. Five times she was questioned, and five times she prayed with him. They were simple, childlike prayers that spoke to his heart. He had had to leave his family back in Bremen, Germany, knowing the city was being bombed.

"I hate this work," he told Corrie.

After the war, Corrie learned that this lieutenant was in an internment camp in Germany. Though her request was not granted, she wrote the following, hoping for his release:

In April 1944, he questioned our family, those who were in prison with us. He knew that most of them were underground workers. He changed my status and tried in several ways to set free my sister and me, but did not succeed because another judge got our trial. He listened with great interest when we spoke of the Gospel and allowed my sister to pray with him. With permission I will take him in our house in Holland for a time with his family.

When Corrie later met Hans Rahms in Germany, she asked him if he had ever recieved Christ as his Savior.

"No, but I could never forget what you told me, or your sister's prayers."

Later that evening, Corrie had the joy of bringing this man, her judge, who could have ordered her execution with one stroke of his pen, to Jesus Christ, our ultimate Judge. Thus was another life touched by Corrie, used of the Lord to sow a seed even in the hell of that prison—a seed she later brought to harvest.

The Bureau of Police, Haarlem, as seen today. It was to this station the ten Boom family was taken when arrested.

Corrie in solitary confinement in Scheveningen prison scratches the date of her arrest on the wall of her cell (from the film THE HIDING PLACE).

While in prison, Corrie received the news that after two days, the Jews had escaped from the Beje's hiding place (from the film THE HIDING PLACE).

Brought before Lt. Hans Rahms for questioning, Corrie is shown incriminating papers that could mean her death and the death of others (from the film THE HIDING PLACE).

Corrie, after the war with Hans Rahms, whom she led to the Lord.

5

Journey to Hell

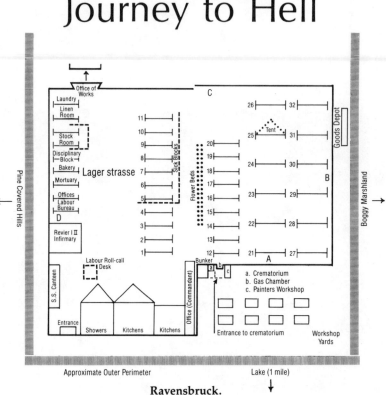

Ravensbruck.

The silence of three months of solitary confinement was broken suddenly by shouts from the guards who were running up and down the corridors.

"Everyone put on their clothing! Get ready to evacuate!"

Corrie excitedly dressed and hastily gathered her few possessions into a pillowcase. The Allies must be near! Her Bible (one Nollie sent) hung in a small pouch on her back under her clothing. Hours went by before another order was given for all prisoners to step into the corridor. Bewildered, they stood there looking at each other for the first time. Corrie was amazed at how many prisoners there were and her eyes traveled up and down the rows looking for one beloved face—Betsie's. There was no sign of her.

Diet Erlich, a gentle, Dutch lady, now living in Grand Rapids, Michigan, remembers that scene clearly.

At the prison in Scheveningen I was in a cell just a few doors from Betsie. We were suddenly ordered to get our things and were taken to a train station near The Hague.

On the platform I actually witnessed the reunion of Betsie and Corrie, after they had been separated for so long. Amid all the terrifying confusion of so many frightened women, they suddenly saw each other. I shall never forget the expressions on their faces! All the pain of separation was for a brief moment forgotten, as they hugged. Still embracing, they were swept into the train, so thankful to the Lord to be together again. For the entire journey they held hands and talked excitedly. The train's destination was Vught, a concentration camp in Holland, from which we hoped we would soon be freed . . . .

Months went by and news filtered in from the outside that the Allies were soon to liberate Holland. Perhaps shortly they would all be going home!

When they heard distant bombing, they dared to hope—but in vain. For two hours Betsie and Corrie listened to the firing squads executing prisoners in the men's camp nearby. Soon after that the prison at Vught was emptied—the prisoners pressed like animals into boxcars for transport into the heart of Germany.

Germany! Was the darkness to triumph? The fear in the boxcars was accentuated by lack of water and food. Eighty women were jammed into a space that humanely could hold forty. Good air was nonexistent. There were no facilities for sanitation. Betsie and Corrie huddled together in the darkness, holding the little Bible.

As the train crossed the border into Germany, the women's hearts sank within them, as they knew they were leaving their homeland, perhaps forever. In one of the boxcars a woman sang:

> Adieu, beloved Netherlands,
> Dear Fatherland, farewell!

Corrie and Betsie felt as if they were on a journey to hell. When the train finally came to its destination and the doors were flung back, they knew they *had* arrived at a hell on *earth—Ravensbruck,* the dreaded concentration camp. It was a terrifying, tragic sight: these women, who had been brutally packed in the train for three days and nights, now being herded toward this place of death with its barbed-wire fences, the concrete buildings, the smoking chimneys of the crematorium. Only a few guards were needed that night. The women were too exhausted, too beaten to even try to escape.

As the gates closed behind her, Corrie wondered if the gates of hell could sound any different. She and Betsie were two out of fourteen hundred women assigned to a building designed to house four hundred, Barracks 28.

Past the scrutiny of the guards, the little Bible made its way into the darkness—a miracle in itself. In the dormitory, protected by fleas and lice so thick the guards would not enter, Corrie and Betsie opened the little book and read the promises of the God who refused to leave man to his own destruction.

Even in this darkness, God used the ten Boom sisters to minister to their fellow sufferers—Corrie able to do so much for people's physical as well as spiritual needs; and Betsie, always frail, now losing strength before Corrie's eyes. But it was Betsie's spiritual strength that gained and radiated through the ghastly surroundings. God had given her His eyes to see beyond the horror and the filth. Like Papa ten Boom the night of his arrest, it was as if angels were shielding Betsie.

Corrie struggled with the promises of God. Did His words really apply . . . the One who said, "I am."

> ". . . I am the light of the world: he that followeth me shall not walk in darkness, but shall have the light of life."
>
> John 8:12 KJV

> ". . . I am come that they might have life, and that they might have it more abundantly."
>
> 10:10

> ". . . I am the resurrection, and the life: he that believeth in me, though he were dead, yet shall he live: And whosoever liveth and believeth in me shall never die . . . ."
>
> 11:25, 26

Then Corrie remembered that God Himself had shown His truth and love in a world that was cruel, just like this. The cross stood out to her, not a thing of failure but of triumph! With Christ's help, she would triumph too, despite this place of degradation.

Corrie performed many acts of sheer bravery. Driven by the overwhelming burden in her heart to bring the message of Christ to all who would listen—protected by Betsie's prayers—she took risks which could have meant death, if she were caught.

One night she learned of a new prisoner—Beatrix Terwind—a young woman of incredible courage, who had flown many missions to England for the underground, saving many lives. Now she had been shot down and captured by the Nazis. They had taken her to the most dreaded barracks of all, one of near-certain death, for there were housed the human beings used in the medical experiments.

Corrie obeyed a leading of the Holy Spirit that she should speak to Beatrix. "Pray for me, Betsie," she whispered, as she darted into the midst of the prisoners who were being marched back to the dreaded barracks. Then she was gone from Betsie's sight.

Inside, Corrie whispered to a woman near her to show which one was Beatrix Terwind. She motioned toward a girl sitting at a table. Corrie went hastily and sat by her side. Quietly, so as not to arouse any suspicion, Corrie started a conversation: "Beatrix, I am Corrie ten Boom—are you in danger of your life?"

Beatrix looked at her with tears in her eyes and nodded.

"Are you prepared to die? Do you know that Jesus died on the cross for the sins of the whole world, also for yours? He loves you."

The young pilot said very gently, "I know!"

Then there was a look of fear on her face. "Corrie, how did you dare to come into this barracks? Do you know they can kill you for that?"

Again her eyes filled with tears. "What a love to have risked your life to tell me this."

Corrie's last words to her: "It is not I; it is Jesus in me. I'll keep praying for you—don't lose heart. Jesus is with you!"

Corrie, deeply moved, left this young woman and climbed out of the bathroom window. Hastily she walked back to her barracks. Betsie was waiting for her return. Corrie, her heart still beating wildly, wondered if her sister had been afraid. "No, I was not. I prayed for you and the Lord gave me peace and assurance that all would be well."

Corrie never saw Beatrix again in Ravensbruck but she continued to pray for her. Years after the war, she learned her prayers had been answered—that this young woman had in fact been spared execution.

"I had to wait at an airport in Holland when I started to think of that brave young woman pilot I'd met in Ravensbruck. I asked an airline stewardess, 'Do you know Beatrix Terwind? Do you know if she ever came out of Ravensbruck?' The girl smiled and said, 'She surely did; she is our head stewardess. Come with me to the office.' There I met Beatrix again—healthy and happy. What a joy to see her under such good circumstances!"

How grateful Corrie was that her Lord used her to bring a touch of comfort to that young pilot, as she sat alone in the bleakness and horror of those barracks.

Stories could be told of so many times that God used Corrie to whisper a few words of encouragement: sometimes to the sick, to the dying, and sometimes to those afraid—not knowing where they would be sent.

Corrie had heard that a group of 250 prisoners were being taken out of the camp to an unknown destination. She could not sleep thinking about them all. She had come to know and love many of them. Was there some word of comfort she could give them? In spite of knowing she could easily be caught, she climbed out of her barracks window. Hiding, she waited for the searchlight to pass her on its rounds, then ran to a place hidden from the guards. From there she could whisper to these prisoners as they went by.

I prayed, "Lord, give me a word for each of them. Perhaps very soon they will die. I cannot do any more for them after they have left." Then the first passed by.

"Jesus is Victor!" I whispered.

"Oh, Corrie—how could you? Go back to your barracks!"

"Fear not. Only believe."

"Thank you, Corrie. God bless you."

"Underneath are the everlasting arms. Jesus has said, *I am with you til the end of the world.* Look to the Lord. He loves you. Jesus is Victor!"

There was joy in my heart as the Holy Spirit gave me a short message for everyone that went through the gate.

When the last of them had gone, Corrie darted back to the barracks, thanking the Lord for giving her the words to say, and for bringing her safely back to Betsie.

One of those prisoners who left Ravensbruck that night told Corrie, years later: "During a tremendous air raid, I was sitting in a corner of a room, as we prisoners were not allowed to go into the bomb shelters. All I could think of were the words you said to us that night as we left Ravensbruck. 'Jesus is Victor!' We were unprotected during the raid, but our building stayed upright. Out of two hundred and fifty prisoners, all returned safely to Holland except one."

Corrie does not think she is courageous. She says, "There was a sense of closeness to the Lord, as I had seldom had before. 'For by thee I have run through a troop; and by my God have I leaped over a wall.' [Psalms 18:29 KJV.] Courage does not depend on our circumstances, but on the relationship that remains during the circumstances."

Each day it seemed that death was all around them. They could never be certain that sunrise would not herald their last day on earth. Corrie recalls: "In the concentration camp sometimes we could have a shower—a hot shower. Oh, what a tremendous blessing! We had to go with many other women into a large, dank room and there would come from the ceiling hundreds of hot showers. Lack of hygiene was one of our sufferings.

"But the terrible thing was that the room was not only a shower room, it was also the gas chamber. When we stood there, we did not know if there would come water or gas.

"At such moments you look death in the eye. You stand, as it were, on the edge of eternity. What a joy it was for me to know that Jesus had brought me the assurance of salvation. If it were gas, then after a short time I would go to the house of the Father, where Jesus is preparing a home for everyone who belongs to Him.

"No, I was not afraid. I could say, 'Death where is thy sting? Where is thy victory?' I praised the Lord for the victory of my Lord Jesus Christ and I felt His hand in my hand."

When Corrie and Betsie were in Ravensbruck, they made many friends. Recently, in a home filled with warmth and hospitality, on the outskirts of Amsterdam, Mimi Lanz Kyzer, a stately woman with white hair and intense, blue eyes, told of the events which led her to meeting the ten Boom sisters.

Mimi had been born into a Swiss doctor's family. Her father began collecting priceless art when they lived in Switzerland. When she was seven years old, her family moved to Amsterdam, where her father had been appointed Professor of Surgery. Their house on the *Museumplein* contained one of the largest private collections of early Italian art. One day it would be given to Holland's renowned Rijks Museum. (During the war the collection came under the greedy eye of Hitler and was sent to Germany. After the war, it was returned safely to the Netherlands.)

In 1944, Mimi Kyzer, caught working in the underground, found herself in a very different world: the horrifying, degrading world of a German concentration camp. It was there the two ten Boom sisters spread a ray of light in Mimi's darkness.

At first I did not want to get to know them. They were with a group of older women and they were always singing hymns! But later, as I began to watch these sisters, I could see something very beautiful about them. They came up to me one day and said, "Hello Swiss. We heard the Germans took your home. Our home in Haarlem is now your home." I was so touched by this. They didn't know me, but they gave me their love and offered me their home!

Because of my doctor father, I was put to work in the camp hospital. There I saw such filth and suffering. Each day I had to assist at the birth of prisoners' babies—often two dozen a day. They were left to die. In Ravensbruck I saw the most heartless, cruel people, but I also saw marvelous people like the ten Booms.

They would preach to us in Dutch and everyone would listen intently. One day Betsie was reading from the Bible, from Psalms 91 ". . . He that dwelleth in the secret place of the most High shall abide under the shadow of the Almighty." As she read, a beautiful shaft of sunlight came into that bleak barracks and rested on her. It was like a ray from heaven. It reminded me of a nineteenth-century painting. There were French, Belgian, Italian, Poles, Russians—everyone was listening. Knowing several languages, I asked one of the prisoners if she understood what Betsie was saying. She said,

"No, we can't, but she says it with her whole heart. *That we under-stand.* We understand the love in her voice." The ten Booms never tried to force their religion on us, they just shared it and lived it.

Mimi Kyzer had many chances to escape while working in the prison hospital, but she knew that if she did, Betsie and Corrie and many others would be vilely punished. Each time someone had managed to get away, there would be terrible beatings and punishments administered to those left behind.

It was to the hospital where Mimi worked that Betsie was brought, desperately ill.

Sweet Betsie died quietly, on December 16, 1944. It was so beautiful how she died—so peacefully, so gently, so radiantly, so ready. Corrie, two other girls, and I walked and walked and walked that night. All of us cried—how we cried! How we loved beautiful Betsie! We were so terribly weak—always cold, always hungry.

The night before Betsie died, she had awakened Corrie. "Corrie, I have to tell you what God has said to me. I am so afraid I will forget one detail!"

Corrie listened as Betsie, her face so emaciated, but so luminous with the love of Christ, went on: "God once said that after the war we must try to get a concentration camp to help homeless people and refugees from Germany. This night He showed me a house in Holland where we must invite the Dutch people who come from concentration camps. Some will find the way to life again in that house. I saw the house in a vision. The most beautiful colors—I saw even the woodwork." Betsie went on to describe the house, the staircase, the garden with its many flowers.

"After we have established it, we must travel over the world, bringing the Gospel. We can tell what God has taught us in this time. We know that from experience Jesus' light is stronger than the deepest darkness. Don't you see that your whole life has been a training for the work you do here, and that you will do after our liberation? It will not be an easy life, always traveling, always with other people, but the Lord will be our strength . . . ."

Mimi Kyzer remembers:

Two weeks after Betsie died, when Corrie was called out of line at roll
call, we did not know whether or not it meant she was going to be
killed. It was terrible.

When her number, 66730, was called, Corrie walked slowly to the
front unafraid, remembering the words of Papa, when as a little girl she
had been afraid of death: ". . . when the time comes that some of us
will have to die, you will look into your heart and find the strength you
need—just in time."

The valley of the shadow of death had no terror for Corrie now.
Jesus had been with her in all her suffering. He would be with her
whatever there was to face.

As Corrie stood there in the bitter, icy weather with others who had
been called, she whispered, "Why am I here?"

"Death sentence," replied a young girl, shivering near her. Corrie
looked at this girl and wondered if she would be the last person she
could tell about Jesus Christ. For three hours they were left standing
there, and for three hours Corrie told of the Love that would be with her
always—she had only to receive it. The prisoners around Corrie listened
too.

The guard came and took Corrie to the office. There she was told she
would be released! *Entlassen!* Released! Her legs, swollen from edema,
kept her from being set free for another eight days. Then, almost unbe-
lieving, she signed the necessary papers—not knowing then that it was a
clerical error that had secured her freedom.

Mimi Kyzer recalls:

When we heard that Corrie had been discharged, we were all thrilled
for her. Everybody loved Corrie. Even the Germans respected her
because she had stamina, her religion, her force, her work. Through
her I realized that unless one had faith one could not last.

The gates of Ravensbruck swung open and Corrie walked out into
freedom.

The "grain of wheat" had "died" in Ravensbruck, and Corrie was now ready for the work God had been preparing her for over the years. The tenderness of the child's heart who had prayed for the unfortunate around her was now completely *His* tenderness. The compassion with which she had reached out to all those in need was now completely *His* compassion. The strength that had kept her in the midst of the hell of Ravensbruck was now *His* strength entirely. And the love that had cared so deeply for her family was now *His* love—the love that cared enough to die for the world.

There was only one thing she would have to learn: the forgiveness that could forgive her betrayers, her enemies. But God would teach this child of His, in the days ahead, the lesson of His Son who, while on the cross, looked down on His enemies and said,

> "Father, forgive them, for they know not what they do . . . ."
>
> Luke 23:34 KJV

Betsie sees Corrie for the first time in months, as they are loaded into the cattle cars, destined for the concentration camp (from the film THE HIDING PLACE).

The prisoners arrive at the dreaded Ravensbruck concentration camp (from the film THE HIDING PLACE).

Interior of Barracks #28, in which 1400 women were crammed; it was designed for only 400 (from the film THE HIDING PLACE).

An actual photo of prisoners in the concentration camp.

From early morning until late into the day, prisoners were made to endure backbreaking work detail (from the film THE HIDING PLACE).

Corrie's number was called out during roll call; she stood there, not knowing if it meant death (from the film THE HIDING PLACE).

An actual alley in Ravensbruck, through which women walked before being shot.

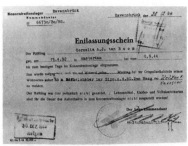

Corrie's discharge paper from Ravensbruck.

With the crematorium smokestack behind her, Corrie walked out into freedom to tell the world that Jesus' light is stronger than the deepest darkness (from the film THE HIDING PLACE).

6

Return to Holland

Tante Corrie with nephew Peter after the war.

For three days Corrie traveled through Germany. She was desperately hungry and thirsty, and her feet were painfully swollen. The journey was agonizing, but each minute was bringing her closer to her beloved homeland!

As the train passed the blackened cities of Germany—Bremen was now one enormous ruin, heaps of rubble where there had once been a beautiful city—Corrie thought of all that had gone before: all the suffering, the heartache of Papa dying, a prisoner, and now, only a few days before, losing her dear sister Betsie. God had spared Corrie for a reason, and she knew that her life was not her own—it was His. He had spoken clearly to Betsie just before she died, and even now there was a longing in Corrie's heart to begin the work He had planned for her.

"Lord, I have received my life back from You. Thank You. Will You tell me how to use it? Give me understanding, a discernment I will need to see everything through Your eyes. My work must be to save souls for eternity, to tell about You. As Paul has said in Second Corinthians 5:20, '. . . to be your personal [representative] . . .' "

As she spoke with her Lord, Corrie realized that money was not important. Neither was honor in the sight of men. She had stood before the smoking chimneys of the crematorium—one step from eternity—and earthly things had taken on a different perspective. There was one thing she longed for—a nice home with good food, music, and the company of others.

As the train finally crossed the border into Holland, Corrie rejoiced! How many times she had wondered if she would ever be able to see this gentle, peace-loving country again. The train came to a halt at Groningen station. Corrie hobbled off the train, her body weak from lack of food during the long journey, and the pain in her feet becoming more and more intense.

Holland had been partially liberated by the Canadians, but Groningen was still under German domination, as was Haarlem. No trains were running there, and Corrie did not know how she would reach her hometown.

She limped to a hospital near the station—it was run by Christians! As she walked through its doors, she felt as if she were experiencing a little bit of heaven on earth. Everyone was so kind. Corrie was no longer used to kindness; she was conditioned to the yells and curses of the cruel guards at Ravensbruck. The nurses here had been trained in loving care toward sick people, and as one came up to greet her, Corrie felt the love of Christ reaching out to her.

Truus Benes, a Dutch nurse, while visiting with Corrie recently, remembered that day:

> I received a telephone call from our Lady Director. She told me there was a woman needing medical help, who had just come from Germany, and was in a pitiful condition. Her name was Corrie ten Boom. The Director told me to see that she had a good meal. I quickly went to where she was waiting, and as we were going to the dining room, I asked her whether she knew a Corrie ten Boom from Haar-

lem. "That's me," Corrie said. "Why, it's Truus Benes! Remember we worked together in the YWCA before the war!" I looked at Corrie in disbelief. To me it was not possible that this could be the woman I had known—so thin, her eyes sunk deep in her face, her hair so unkempt. Then Corrie saw herself in a mirror and said, "It is no miracle you don't recognize me—I look strange."

I could not believe my eyes . . . I reached out and touched her sore, chapped hands and said, "It *is* you!" How we laughed together! I took her to the dining room and put a meal in front of her. I have never seen anyone eat like Corrie did that day!

Corrie remembers that meal, her first after Ravensbruck, served to her on a white tablecloth: "It was a little bit as if I came from hell into heaven, surrounded by those who had been trained in being good to people. That first meal . . . oh, I will never forget it, never! It was brussel sprouts, potatoes, meat and gravy, pudding with currant juice, and apple sauce. Then Truus took me and let me have a long, hot bath!"

"Oh, yes, I remember," recalls Truus. "You were like a baby, loving that bath. It was hard to get you out of it. Your poor scab-crusted skin and your feet, so swollen—how good it felt to you."

The nurses found clean clothing to outfit Corrie in her first hours of freedom. Several nurses had been former leaders of the Netherlands Girls' Clubs, and remembered her with great affection. Corrie says: "They dressed me up as if I were a doll. One of them had lingerie, another shoes, another a dress, and pins for my hair. I felt so happy I laughed for sheer joy. How sweet they were to me."

Truus took Corrie to a bright, colorful room with a bed—with clean, white sheets! The filth of Ravensbruck was far behind her now, as she lay her weary head on the soft, white pillow. Her eyes drank in thirstily the bright colors in the room . . . the curtains, the bedspread . . . she had been starved for color in the concentration camp. Gone was the gray that had dominated her life. A young nurse brought a pillow and gently placed it under Corrie's swollen feet.

The pillow under Corrie's weary head was wet with her tears, as she thanked the Lord for His goodness. The sounds of cruelty were gone, and in their place she could hear, through the open window, sounds of children playing happily and bells in the distance, chiming the passing of time.

Corrie gradually regained her strength. After ten days, transportation was arranged for her to travel home through underground sources, since there were no trains running to Haarlem.

As she crossed Haarlem's Spaarne River, the welcoming sight of Saint Bavo's greeted her. She was home! Turning into the Barteljorisstraat her heart began to beat faster, as she saw the Beje. There were tears in her eyes, as she walked toward it—memories of the family welled up. It seemed she could hear their voices coming from the windows—Peter playing the piano . . . .

There her sister Nollie stood in the doorway of the Beje. Hugging, they laughed and cried together. Corrie ran her hand lovingly over the door leading into the watch shop, and as she walked past his workbench, her heart ached for her beloved Papa. She paused before the old clock. The last time it had been wound was by Papa, as he was being led off to prison. Her rough, calloused hands gently pulled the weights, setting it once more in motion.

Corrie's life slowly began to return to a form of normalcy. Her "fellow gangsters" as she called her former underground workers, had collected six hundred guilders for her, so that she could begin life again.

She was still a marked woman, however. Only recently a Dutchman told this story:

> Corrie was marked for assassination. A young Dutch girl who worked with Corrie got word of the plot. An N.S.B. woman [a Dutch Nazi] invited Corrie to her home, under the guise of protecting her. The young Dutch girl knew the woman was a traitor and told Corrie that, if she went, she would be killed. A few days later, the N.S.B. woman was riding down a street on her bicycle. Mysteriously, a shot rang out and the woman was killed. Corrie was grieved to hear this.

Though the war was not yet over, the underground workers encouraged Corrie not to work with them anymore, as they knew she was constantly being watched. She agreed.

The watch shop reopened. Corrie again took in outsiders—this time mentally retarded people came to her home for care and protection. Her days were full and busy again. Life was hard for the Hollanders though. The Dutch people were still eating their tulip bulbs to ward off starvation—most of their food was shipped to Germany.

Corrie found she was still weak and could not walk properly, but her thinking was clear, and she longed to share the blessings that the Lord had taught her. She began to speak in churches of many different denominations—meeting so many Christians who had prayed for her while she was in prison. These meetings had to be held in secret, and each time someone would come in while Corrie was speaking, she would switch her talk to one on the care of the mentally retarded, until she was sure the person could be trusted.

Even though Corrie's days were busy and filled with people, there was something—someone—whom she missed almost unbearably. One night as Corrie made her way back down the alley outside the Beje, she suddenly knew who that person was. She realized just how much she missed Betsie—Betsie who had been her playmate, her sister, her friend, and in Ravensbruck, her spiritual mother. But Betsie was gone forever. All that remained were those words Betsie had said to her in Ravensbruck:

> We must tell people what we have learned . . . that no darkness can keep out God's marvelous light. They will believe us, because we've been here.

At that moment the Beje ceased to be home for Corrie ten Boom. The Lord had other plans for her.

Pamela Rosewell (left) with Truus Benes, the nurse who first helped Corrie when she was released from Ravensbruck.

Corrie in Haarlem, overlooking one of its many canals.

Sitting by her favorite clock— the one that Papa stopped
to wind as he was being taken from the Beje to prison.

Standing in the Grote Markt with Saint Bavo's in the background.

With Peter, going through a trunk full of the ten Boom memorabilia, including letters written from concentration camp.

As he once did for all the ten Booms, Peter plays the organ for his Tante Corrie.

7

Rebuilding Lives

On the grounds of "Schapenduinen," where God used Corrie to heal broken lives.

God led Corrie to one of the most beautiful homes in Holland named *Schapenduinen*, located in Bloemendaal. The elderly lady who owned it allowed Corrie to rent a part of this large mansion. Corrie raised funds for the project, as she spoke all over Holland. With the help of many people who gave furniture and clothing, the house was prepared for those who would so desperately need the solace of its walls. When the war ended in May 1945, she began the work of rehabilitating ex-prisoners. To Schapenduinen they came—from the concentration camps and from the attics and cellars of Dutch homes, where they had been hiding such a long time. The scars of their wartime experiences were gradually healed in this place of peace and Christian caring.

One who came to help Corrie was Diet Erlich, who had been with her and Betsie in Scheveningen and Vught. She recalls:

> During the war I had been engaged to a wonderful, young man, who was the leader of our Christian group. We had just taken out our wedding license, my wedding dress was hanging in my closet—when we were arrested. He was dragged from one camp to another. I endured the horrors of Scheveningen and Vught, longing for the day when we would be together again. After the war I learned that he had been killed in Dachau . . . this was such a terrible, terrible blow to me.
>
> Then Corrie heard about it and right away she sent a message to me which simply said, "I need you," and she asked me to come to the beautiful rehabilitation home. She had said, "I need you—to help prepare for the people who are coming back from Germany," but really it was to help me get over the war and my great loss. This is so typical of Corrie. Caring for others enabled me to go on and find a purpose for living.

Lotte Reimeringer came to Bloemendaal to help Corrie run this God-given project. Now living in California, she remembers the days there:

> The house was called *Schapenduinen*, which means "sheep dunes," and I think it was a wonderful name, because many lost sheep were found by the Lord in that house. The house was very much like Betsie had seen in the vision shortly before she died—the beautiful staircase, the large rooms with lovely furniture, and it was in a park, so it was wonderful for the people who had to recuperate—they could walk in the beautiful gardens.

One of those who found healing from the ravages of their wartime experiences was a young Jewish girl. Recently, in a voice choked with emotion, the now-grown woman told of her days there:

> When my mother and I returned from Belsen concentration camp in 1945, both of us were skin and bones—really not like human beings anymore. We did not know how to start a normal life again. Then we heard about the convalescent home, which had been established through the initiative of Tante Corrie. My mother was ac-

cepted into the home gravely ill, and it was Tante Corrie who nursed
her back into being a human being again.

When we were first brought there, we told Tante Corrie that we
had no money and she said, "It does not matter. Money is not important, just come." We were there for six months.

Finding it difficult to go on, the woman whispered, "It was Corrie ten
Boom who gave me back my mother!"

Healing came slowly to the guests. Corrie refused to set curfews or
restrict them in any way. Their lives had known such harshness and
deprivation, strict discipline did not play any part in Corrie's "therapy."
Part of that was encouraging them to enjoy music. Friends came often to
give concerts, and Corrie tried to give the guests a love for Bach.

As Betsie had seen, the best therapy was working in the gardens.
The talk of crops replaced the bitter recriminations. Corrie was certain of
a person's healing when he was able to forgive. It seemed for each one,
there was a cruel guard, an enemy, or a traitor at home who had to be
forgiven. Often it was the Dutch who had assisted the Nazis who were
the hardest for people to forgive. They were now the harassed and
hunted ones. They were turned out of their homes and were unable to
find work. Attempts to bring them to Bloemendaal failed, for the hatred
of them ran so deep. Although few people could understand why, Corrie
turned the Beje over to some of them who needed a home. This act of
charity was not appreciated by her neighbors. It is not often the world
actually sees someone obeying the words of Jesus:

> "But I say unto you, Love your enemies, bless them
> that curse you, do good to them that hate you, and
> pray for them which despitefully use you, and perse-
> cute you."
>
> Matthew 5:44 KJV

Schapenduinen was a place where people could find healing not
only for their bodies, but their souls too. Lotte Reimeringer recalls:

> Corrie was not only concerned about older people, but also the
> younger ones. After the war, the Youth for Christ organization was
> having many meetings, and hundreds of people were coming to the

Lord. It was necessary that follow-up work be done, so Corrie made the home available. About fifty or sixty young people came there for Bible study, prayer, fellowship, and singing.

Spencer DeJong, one of the ministers at Melodyland Christian Center in California, remembers very vividly those times:

> My mind goes back to Holland in 1946, when our Youth for Christ team arrived in Amsterdam to begin two months of evangelistic meetings in that wonderful country. It was right after World War II, and there were ruins everywhere, due to the bombings and Nazi attacks. Our team was the first one to go out under Youth for Christ, and how well I remember Corrie opening Schapenduinen to us, where she housed so many homeless people of the Netherlands. Her help and cooperation were so valuable, as we launched out to preach in thirty-nine cities in the Netherlands.
>
> I have treasured her friendship and love so very, very much over the years. Corrie has been such a great blessing to me and to countless thousands.

With the work in the rehabilitation home in Bloemendaal well organized, Corrie was able to accept some of the many speaking engagements coming to her. She traveled to other cities in Holland, throughout Europe, and to the United States.

It was while Corrie was in America that she received a letter from her board in Holland, telling her that a house was for sale called *Zonneduin* where the rehabilitation work could continue. Corrie said, "I wrote back, 'Buy it immediately.' The board wrote, 'Do you think money is falling from heaven?' I wrote, 'That is the only address I expect it from!' " God sent the money and Zonneduin was purchased.

Corrie continued her travels, which led her back to Germany—a country she hoped she would never have to see again. But the biggest wounds were *in* Germany. Corrie could see it in people's eyes—the guilt, the shame, the darkness. The atmosphere was one of defeat and hopelessness.

After speaking at a meeting in Berlin one evening, a tall German man came up to Corrie and asked to speak with her. Hesitatingly, his head down, he began: "I was one of the guards of Ravensbruck—I was there at the time you were a prisoner. Last Christmas I accepted Jesus Christ as my Savior. I repented of my sins but then I prayed, *God, give me the opportunity to ask one of my victims for forgiveness!* That is why I am here. Will you forgive me?"

This was a testing time for Corrie. She had taught the people being rehabilitated at the house in Bloemendaal that true healing could only come when they forgave their enemies. As she stood face-to-face with one of *her* former enemies, she found that deep in her heart she still had not forgiven all that had happened in the past.

Corrie looked into the face of this man standing there in a dark gray overcoat—the very color reminded her of Ravensbruck. As she remembered from the past his uniform and the peaked hat with the skull and crossbones insignia barbarically displayed, a coldness came into her heart. Memories of Betsie and the degradation of their sufferings flooded into her mind. There was no forgiveness in her for this man.

Then she prayed: *Jesus help me! I can lift my hand. I can do that much. You supply the feeling.*

With difficulty, Corrie put her hand into her former guard's hand and instantly a miraculous thing happened. A warmth shot down her arm into her hand, the warmth of the healing power of the Holy Spirit. It brought tears to her eyes and she said:

"I forgive you with all of my heart!"

In Darmstadt, Germany, Corrie rented a former concentration camp. She remembered Betsie's words to her: "These are now used to destroy people. We must ask God to give us one and we can use it to build up lives."

The barbed wire came down; window boxes appeared; green paint covered gray. Corrie has said, "Betsie never saw the flowers—the beautiful colors in the house that God gave in Holland after the war. She did not see the camp I arranged with my friends in Germany. But when I went to look at her that night she died in Ravensbruck, there was an expression of heavenly beauty and perfect peace on her face. Had she seen the flowers and beautiful colors before her body died?"

At Darmstadt, Corrie learned the value of listening. As she sat or walked with the people who came, God revealed the tender spot where His love could be applied and understood.

Corrie saw a haggard woman sitting in a corner, completely dejected. She found out that the woman had been a professor of music at the Dresden Conservatory. Corrie's love for Bach was able to touch this despondent human being. When she asked the woman to play one of his most difficult compositions, it touched a spot in her heart. Seated at a broken-down piano, she realized, as the notes poured out this beautiful melody of Bach's, she had lost everything except that which mattered to her most—her music. Corrie showed her the precious wealth she still retained and helped her see the riches of knowing the Son of God—of receiving within her His love and grace.

The Canadians liberate Haarlem, 1945.

Diet Erlich and Corrie, who were in concentration camp and Schapenduinen together, reminisce years later.

Corrie teaches a Bible study to a group
at the rehabilitation center.

Lotte Reimeringer plays the piano
for guests at Schapenduinen.

Papa's portrait presides over a songfest.

Some of the woodwork Betsie spoke of, when she had
a vision of Schapenduinen while at Ravensbruck.

Corrie visits with her "angels" many years after the war, when Schapenduinen was used as a home for mentally retarded.

A concentration camp barracks during the war.

Corrie with one of the Lutheran Sisterhood of Mary, who helped her convert Darmstadt concentration camp into a haven for refugees.

A former camp at Darmstadt, converted by Corrie, with bright colors and flowers.

8
To the World

At an orphanage in the Congo.

It was at this time of her life that Corrie literally became "a tramp for the Lord"—a name she called herself. Invitations came from around the world, until it seemed they would overwhelm her. Traveling was difficult for her at her age, always staying in other people's homes. One day she found herself in a bedroom where there was no writing table—a necessity for Corrie who had so much correspondence to answer. She was inundated with requests to speak. She spread all the letters on her bed and after looking at them, decided she would return to Holland to minister there full time. It would be so much easier; she could sleep in her own bed each night—no more packing, no more traveling.

Then Corrie picked up her Bible, which had been her guidebook for so long, and asked the Lord for His message for her. She said: "I asked Him, 'Lord, what would You have me do?' I opened the Book of Romans, chapter 10 verse 14: 'How then shall they call on him in whom they have not believed? and how shall they believe in him of whom they have not heard? and how shall they hear without a preacher?'

"I sat for a long time, thinking . . . . It is not our task to give God instructions. We are simply to report for duty."

Corrie obeyed the call of God and *He* gave her the strength and grace to continue her travels.

Corrie went to Taiwan and worked there with Lillian Dixon with her leprosy patients, ministering to the dire needs of these lonely, ostracized people.

In India, a woman came to Corrie and asked her to pray for healing. Corrie laid hands on her, never knowing that this woman had leprosy. Years later, the woman met Corrie again—she had been completely healed.

To others Corrie brought the most precious of God's healings, that of the spirit. In Argentina, she visited a hospital where a polio epidemic had left wards full of people in iron lungs. Her first reaction was to leave the ward and cry. She told the Lord she was unable to speak to these people, but she received the same answer she had received many times before from Him, "I know *you* cannot, but I can!" With that assurance she went from patient to patient, telling them about the Lord Jesus Christ who breathes into each one of us His Holy Spirit.

Corrie spoke all over America. While she was in Grand Rapids, Michigan, she came in contact with her old friend from Vught, Diet Erlich. Recently, as she recalled her reunion with Corrie, Diet showed no signs of the agony she had gone through in the notorious death camp:

> Corrie came here to Grand Rapids and spoke to about ten thousand people, telling of the faithfulness and love of God, even in prison. Over the years I had not been able to talk about it. It was a chapter in my life I wanted to forget. I had closed the door on the past and did not want to think about it any more.
>
> When Corrie spoke with such courage and love, she really touched me. I began to feel terribly guilty. I went to church the next

Sunday, and the preacher spoke on the ten lepers; they didn't talk about what the Lord had done in healing them and only one said, "Thank You."

That next week, when the news got out that I knew Corrie, I was asked to speak to our ladies' group. They insisted, and reluctantly I accepted. That first time I found it very difficult to talk without crying, but since then I have had many opportunities to share God's goodness in my life.

Corrie really touched my life, and I am very thankful to the Lord for her and for His love.

While Corrie was speaking in England, the Lord answered one of her most fervent prayers. She needed someone to help her, to be her companion on the wearing trips she was making all over the world. Her correspondence was becoming impossible for her to cope with by herself. Corrie met Conny van Hoogstraten, a Dutch student studying at a Bible school. Her father had been a missionary in Indonesia and had died in a Japanese prison camp. Conny and the rest of her family were in prison there for three years, so instantly there was a rapport between the two women.

Conny traveled all over the world with Corrie. They prayed together, worked together, laughed together, and Corrie wondered how she had ever managed without her. As she spoke to the crowds, she would look out and know that Conny was praying for her.

After several years, Conny came to Corrie to tell her that the Lord had brought someone into her life, and that she was getting married. It was difficult for Corrie to have to let this young woman go. By now Corrie's only remaining sister, Nollie, had died and Conny had become like "family" to her. Together they prayed that the Lord would bring someone to replace Conny. The Lord answered by giving Corrie a new secretary in the person of Ellen de Kroon, a striking blond, Dutch nurse.

(Only two years after Conny married, she became ill—cancer was diagnosed. Corrie says: "Conny died a victorious death. Her life bore much fruit, and she prepared many people to meet the Master, our Lord Jesus Christ, who came to call her home to be with Him forever.")

Ellen de Kroon endeared herself to Corrie, the first time they met. It was her unconscious gesture of concern for Corrie's well-being—a simple thing like a shawl placed around her shoulders, when she thought Corrie might be feeling the chill of evening—that was a testimony of God's love reaching out through Ellen. This began nine years of serving the Lord together all over the world. Ellen became like a daughter to Corrie. In 1976 Ellen married Robert Stamps, a chaplain at Oral Roberts University, and it was Tante Corrie who gave away "A daughter in marriage."

Ellen remembers her years with Tante Corrie and speaks of Corrie with great affection:

> Tante Corrie's life was very creative. I remember the first week I worked with her, I found in her closet a little piece of cloth. I was ready to throw it away, when I saw something on it. It was a piece of embroidery that Tante Corrie did when she was all alone in prison. She had one needle and she pulled some threads and made a beautiful flower. That is Tante Corrie exactly.
>
> I remember also a time when we were going to Hungary. God told Tante Corrie to go and she said, "We are going." We had to order our tickets and everything went well, until the man at the travel agency called and said, "Ellen, you have got your visa, but Tante Corrie didn't get hers."
>
> I had to learn the beautiful lesson of trust. Tante Corrie trusted God in everything, even in disappointments. When Tante Corrie heard she could not go, she knew God had another door. That very same week we got a package of books. In it was Tante Corrie's book *A Prisoner and Yet*, translated into the language of the people of Hungary. Tante Corrie thought she had to go, but God had a different way, and she prayed and thanked God for the new open door.
>
> *Trust in God* . . . that is the beautiful lesson I have learned from Tante Corrie.

Knowing the darkness of being behind bars, Corrie entered prison doors in more than forty countries. In Manila she spoke to five thousand prisoners, many awaiting the death sentence. Corrie was able to minister to these men—in

Ravensbruck she too had looked death in the face, but had not been afraid because of Jesus.

In Africa, she spoke to a political prisoner on death row, a young man named Kimio, who seethed with hatred for his enemies. Because Corrie had found the secret of forgiveness when she'd faced the guard from Ravensbruck, she showed this man the way to God's grace. Through her words, God poured the freedom of forgiveness and the joy of the Holy Spirit. The darkest, most overcrowded, dismal prisons in Africa were not immune.

God also led Corrie behind the Iron Curtain. He was near as the customs official, seeing how old Corrie was, carried her Bible-filled suitcase to a waiting taxi, never knowing its precious contents! To the people of Russia, Siberia, Poland, East Germany, and Czechoslovakia she brought the message that would free them spiritually. There she met many wonderful Christians, who rejoiced to meet this woman of God. Through her, the Lord Jesus assaulted the enemy lines and set many captives free.

To war-torn Vietnam Corrie went with Brother Andrew, a man whom God has used so tremendously to spread the Word in many Communist countries. Behind the lines, to the hospitals, on the planes, this team carried the good news of Jesus Christ.

In Holland recently, Brother Andrew recalled those days of Corrie's willingness to serve regardless of the cost:

In Saigon I remember Corrie, who was then seventy-five, speaking at a Youth Rally. They called her "double old grandmother," a form of endearment. I had been in the northern part of Vietnam with the tribes, behind the Viet Cong lines. I flew down to be with her to celebrate her birthday. How surprised she was when, in the evening meeting, everyone sang "Happy Birthday" to her! We had also gone out and bought her a big bunch of flowers.

On that same trip, while on a plane, I was reading an American newspaper which had a report on the war activities in Vietnam. I came across the well-known military phrase "search and destroy." Suddenly it struck me, and I could have cried. I could visualize the soldiers going in to search for people and then to kill them. I handed the paper to Corrie and said, "Read that and tell me what you think." After reading it she gave me a verse, the same one I was thinking of [see Luke 19:10]:

"Jesus said, 'I am come to seek and to save that which was lost.' " Jesus' mission: to seek and to save; man's mission: to search and destroy. This is how we began our ministry together in Vietnam—to seek and to save that which is lost. Many came to the Lord—American soldiers, marines, tribesmen, Chinese, Vietnamese.

Brother Andrew went on to say that the trip was a tremendous strain on Corrie emotionally. The shooting, the bombing, war planes flying low overhead brought back painful memories of the war and the concentration camp. Physically she was very weak, and nearly every morning Brother Andrew would have to go to her room to pray with her for healing—for strength and energy even to get up and do a good day's work.

Brother Andrew continued:

Once she was up she was remarkable. I sure admired that old soldier of Jesus Christ there in Vietnam, in the bush with the troops, in the planes. The Lord really used her.

While in Vietnam their interpreter, a young man named Do Van Nguyen, endeared himself greatly to Corrie. Over the years a beautiful relationship developed. Do has a deep love for Corrie, and she returns this love, calling him "my son Do." He expressed his feelings for her in this way:

When Corrie came to Vietnam in 1967 with Brother Andrew, she asked me to interpret. While she was preaching, I came under deep conviction to commit my life to the Lord. I went to Bible school and later became a pastor of a church.

Many things impressed me about Corrie's coming to Vietnam. The war was spreading, and people fled from one town to another with fear and frustration. Here was a person who was not an enemy, who came from a peaceful country, and traveled half way around the world to share with them the Gospel of peace, of joy, of hope—and at her age. Most of the young people, including myself, had run away from any Christian work, any service for the Lord. But here was a lady who came bravely to us with love flowing out of her eyes and her heart, to preach to us . . . to share with us the Gospel of peace and love. Her messages stirred up my heart and so I said to the Lord, "Here is my life, take it and may it be a blessing to many of the refugees in the land and anywhere You lead me."

By the grace of God, when the Communists took over, I was able to bring my family and eighty-three members of my church to this beautiful land, America. Corrie's organization has helped finance the work in Portland, Oregon. But it is her heart, her prayers, and her devoted work for the Vietnamese people that have touched so many of us. Each time I received a new refugee, I'd report to her over the telephone and she always praised the Lord."

As Corrie has traveled all over the world, she has shown her great love for children. Sensing that love, they have responded to her. While she was in Vietnam, news traveled fast that Corrie ten Boom had bought a slave! She had paid forty dollars and bought a little boy named Jech!

Here in Corrie's words is what actually happened: "Jech and his brothers and sisters had all been sold into bondage because of an overwhelming debt incurred by his parents. I was able to 'purchase' his freedom, and he was placed in an orphanage."

Corrie adopted Jech—his big brown eyes dancing with mischief—who no doubt reminded Corrie of herself when she was young!

One day she was looking out of the window of a house in Vietnam and saw Jech running across the garden to a boundary fence, following a playmate. Just as he was about to climb through the fence, Jech stopped, turned around, and came back.

When Corrie asked him why he had changed his mind, Jech said: "My friend had asked me to go with him. We were going to do something naughty. Just as I got to the fence I thought, 'Mom is praying for me,' and I had to turn around and come back.''

When the Communists took over Vietnam, the orphanage where little Jech was being cared for fell under their control. Corrie does not know what happened to her little adopted son, but she has continued praying for him and thousands like him. Her influence touched that young life and God has promised that His Word will not return void. In the days ahead, perhaps not here, but one day in heaven, Corrie and her little boy will be reunited.

Among her many invitations to speak all over the world was one asking her to address a convention that was to be held in Jerusalem. One of her traveling companions at that time was Hans Moolenburgh, a tall, vital doctor from Holland. He remembers first hearing of Corrie ten Boom:

I was talking to my assistant about the Christian life and how people we call "saints" are not really saints in real life. My assistant said, "There is one exception to what you say—Corrie ten Boom." I had never heard of her.

Corrie was speaking in Haarlem the next week, and so I went to hear her. She spoke to three hundred Haarlem youth from the ages of thirteen to seventeen, a most difficult audience. They listened for one and a half hours—spellbound. I was fascinated by her, too. She had such a love; it radiated from her. I loved her at first sight.

That meeting was in 1974 and was the beginning of our friendship. Later she called and asked if I would accompany her on the trip to Jerusalem. "I want my doctor to go with me. I don't feel safe without my doctor."

So I went. On the plane, once we were in the air, I said, "Do you feel safe now, Corrie?"

"Don't talk rubbish," she said with mock indignation, "I always feel safe. You needed a vacation. You looked so pale." Her eyes were twinkling like a small child's.

In Jerusalem she spoke to the people for one hour. When she sat down, she said to me, "I stopped talking because all these people are so tired!"

Actually Tante Corrie did become ill while we were in Jerusalem and needed my services. Her body was always hurting somewhere, but she would not give in. She prayed, then went to speak.

During this time together in Jerusalem, the Lord used Corrie to calm fears that had long plagued Hans Moolenburgh.

It seemed that I was always searching for Jesus. I had come from a liberal family. I knew a lot about the Bible, but more like a scribe than a Christian. I read about it, talked to people about it, heard preachers, but always thinking to myself, "Where is Jesus? I know He is the Son of God and must be the Savior of my life." I knew this in my head, but something in my heart stayed cold. The problem mounted all through the years.

When I was with Corrie, sitting in the hot Jerusalem sun, I told her my problem.

She said, "Why is this?"

I said, "Tante Corrie, I simply don't know."

"Then we'd better ask the Lord—right away. This simply can't be." So we prayed.

Then I saw what it was. *I was afraid to be tortured for my faith.* I told Corrie I had seen many people who had been tortured. "I am afraid we will have occupation again, and that I will be taken to prison and will have to choose between the Lord and torture." I felt that when I am absolutely in Christ this will happen. I am not a very brave man and I believed that this is what was keeping me back.

She didn't look down at me; didn't despise me; didn't say anything nasty—I am still emotional when I tell this—she said, "How I understand *you!*"

"Why me?"

"Because you are a doctor. You have heard all the stories about torture. You've seen people in pain. So if anyone can imagine what it is, then it is you. Of *course* this is your problem."

Then she told me the story her father had told her when she was afraid of death as a little girl . . . that when she was going on a journey, he didn't give her the train ticket, until she arrived at the station . . . I knew then that the Lord would give me the courage, if I ever needed it. I gave in. That was the turning point and I met the Lord there. . . .

Because Corrie knew what it was to be afraid and the Lord had given her His comfort, she did not look down at this doctor who confessed his fears.

The "grain of wheat" knew how she would have responded without the Lord's courage in her heart, and so she did not judge.

Corrie and Betsie. Truly they went around the world with the message God gave them, through Betsie's vision.

Corrie with letters from all over the world, requesting her to speak.

In 1952 Corrie speaks in Saigon.

Corrie's "mink" (which wasn't mink!) served as a blanket, and the large pockets were crammed with necessities, as she tramped for the Lord. Here she is in America.

Corrie with her first secretary and traveling companion, Conny van Hoogstraten.

With a group of young people at Capenwray Hall in England.

With a Greek Orthodox priest.

Corrie holds child in Kumbya, 1962.

With Reverend Doss in Madras.

At the Taj Mahal, India.

Ellen de Kroon with Corrie in Holland.

Corrie speaks behind the Iron Curtain. Ellen is seated in the front row.

With Ellen and a group of Operation Mobilization young people in Holland.

With Brother Andrew in Vietnam.

In Da Nang, Vietnam.

Corrie's adopted son, Jech, hugged by a friend in Vietnam.

Pastor Do Van Nguyen of Vietnam, who now lives in the USA with his family.

Corrie and friends in Russia.

Corrie with elderly woman near Siberia.

In Vietnam.

Speaking to a group near Siberia.

With some friends in a Communist country.

Speaking at a Billy Graham Crusade.

Corrie with a group at an International Congress on Evangelism, Lausanne, Switzerland. Standing: Dr. Grady Wilson, Dr. and Mrs. Walter Smyth, Dr. Roy McKeown, Dr. Ted Engstrom, Dr. Bob Findley, the Palermo brothers, Dr. Harold Ockenga, Dr. Bob Pierce, Dr. Bob Evans, George Wilson, T. W. Wilson, Rev. Greg Tingson, Cliff Barrows. Seated: Corrie, Mrs. Ralph Neighbor, Billy Graham, Dr. Vasersnoot.

With her nephew Peter, now an evangelist, in Switzerland.

With Art Linkletter at a Hollywood gathering. Ruth Graham and Bill Brown in the background.

On Ellen's wedding day.

Corrie gives the message.

Tramp for the Lord heads for her next destination.

9

Corrie Honored

Plaque commemorating hiding-place site.

The woman who had come from such humble beginnings was invited to stay in the palace of her Queen after the war. For an hour each evening, Corrie sat with Queen Wilhelmina, discussing the Bible and praying together. She has never been one to seek honor or attention, and she did not feel any more elated sharing the Scriptures with her Queen than when she was teaching one of the mentally retarded children she loved so much.

While Corrie was speaking at a Faith at Work Camp on April 17, 1962, she was handed an official-looking document which had been sent her by Queen Juliana of the Netherlands. This made her a Knight of the highest order in Holland. The audience cheered, delighted that she had received this for her courageous work during World War II. As she stood looking at the document, Corrie remembered that her father, the "Grand Old Man of Haarlem," had also received the same title from Queen Wilhelmina before the war.

While holding the formal announcement in the most informal setting of a campground, Corrie was serenaded by the audience singing "There Is Nothing Like a Dame!"

The wife of the Minister of Justice for the Netherlands, who was responsible for seeing that Corrie was given the knighthood, had met Corrie in 1953 at an International Congress, and they became very close friends. Her name is Mrs. Elly Beerman-de Roos, and in Holland she told of that friendship:

> Corrie is one of the children of God with whom I have no difficulties. We have been a blessing to each other. We have been able to take each other's criticism. I would share with Corrie what I thought she should hear, and she would listen. Corrie often rebuked me about things in my life too!

Apart from the spiritual bond these two women have, it is their sense of humor, too, that has made them such close friends for twenty-five years.

> We have always laughed together. I would say to Corrie, "Oh, how silly you are,"and Corrie would respond in her own inimitable fashion, only as she can respond with her own keen sense of humor!
>
> We have both had unhappy experiences in our lives but we both agree that we must open our hearts and love. "Love your enemies" is one of the great things in our lives. We both know that we cannot do this with our own natures. We must be reborn. Corrie has been a confirmation of this in my life.
>
> In America, the people often seem more interested in Corrie's history. But it is so important that we all learn the deep lessons from her experiences.

Many other honors have been bestowed upon Corrie. She has received a doctorate of literature from Gordon College in Wenham, Massachussetts. Awards have been given her by cities and church and civic organizations. She has had schools and babies named after her—even an iguana!

Mrs. Thelma Elfstrom, a close friend of Corrie's in America, laughingly remembers when the news came to Corrie, telling her she had had a bulldog named after her!

> Corrie is full of little surprises, when you least expect them. Her friends Fran and Mike Ewing and I were visiting Corrie. She had just received a letter from a woman who told her that she had named her highly prized, pedigreed bulldog "Corrie" in her honor . . . so we all began to tease her. Suddenly, with that well-known twinkle in her eyes, she began to bark . . . and she kept it up, until we were all in stitches!

In 1975, because of the tremendous interest Corrie's books had stirred in the Beje, she decided to open it as a museum. Visitors flocked there and stood in reverent wonder, as they looked at the little house which God had used to protect so many Jews. The narrow, winding stairs creaked and groaned under the weight of so many visitors.

Standing in the living room the visitor could imagine the happy ten Boom family gathered around the oval table, the center of laughter and the tears of so many years of family living; imagine Papa reading the Bible and praying for the needs of the world. The actual hiding place was reconstructed.

The Sisters of Mary from Darmstadt (who together with Corrie had converted a concentration camp into a place of peace and rehabilitation for the tortured, bewildered refugees) gave a plaque to be hung in the Beje, so that all who visited could see their contrition for what the Nazis had done to so many Dutch people. It reads:

> Have mercy on me, O God,
> according to thy steadfast love;
> according to thy abundant mercy
> blot out my trangressions.
> Wash me thoroughly from my iniquity,
> and cleanse me from my sin!
> For I know my transgressions,
> and my sin is ever before me.
>
>   Psalms 51:1–3 [RSV]

MAY THIS PLAQUE BE AN EXPRESSION OF OUR SHAME AND GRIEF OVER THE SERIOUS CRIME THAT OUR GERMAN PEOPLE COMMITTED AGAINST HOLLAND DURING WORLD WAR II. MAY IT ALSO BE A TOKEN OF LOVE AND GRATITUDE TO THE DUTCH PEOPLE WHO ASSISTED THE JEWS WHILE THEY WERE BEING PERSECUTED, AND WHO RESPONDED TO THE INJUSTICES OF OUR GERMAN NATION BY SHOWING GOODNESS TO GOD'S CHOSEN PEOPLE.

GOD BLESS HOLLAND!
The Evangelical Sisterhood of Mary
November 1975, Darmstadt, West Germany

The Beje finally had to have its doors closed because the flow of visitors became too much to cope with safely. Corrie was sorry to have to disappoint so many people, who came from all over the world, by closing it. As she said, "It was closed because of too much success!"

An honor that is dear to Corrie's heart was given to her in Flagstaff, Arizona. She has a great concern and love for the American Indians and on July 4, 1977, she was honored by a group of several hundred Christian Indians who had gathered for a pow-wow. The President of CHIEF (Christian Hope Indian Eskimo Fellowship) Tom Claus, a Mohawk Indian, came forward to address Corrie:

I want you to know that we accept you as an Indian; you are our blood sister, and you are our spiritual sister in Jesus Christ.

When we bestow an Indian name, it is the highest honor we can give. When your name was nominated to our CHIEF committee we thought that we would like to pick a name that is really meaningful to you, Corrie.

We realize that in the past you have identified with the Jews in their suffering—now you have identified with American Indians in our plight. Even though you have been on the front line of battle and have seen bloodshed and war, you have always been a demonstration of God's love. That is why we give you the name *Loma-Si*, which is Hopi for "beautiful flower," because you are one of God's beautiful flowers. We do thank God for you . . . .

Tom Claus then presented Corrie with a magnificent Indian headdress with CORRIE embroidered in beads across the front of it. A beautiful shawl, made by a woman from the Kiowa tribe, was given to her also. On it was a cross and an arrow going around it, signifying that in Christ we have eternal life.

Corrie, in her speech thanking them, said:

> To be a member of your tribes makes me so happy, and it is for me a little foretaste of heaven, when I will be united with all the tribes of the world, when we will be gathered around Jesus Christ . . . .

(Corrie made a colorful film sharing the Gospel with American Indians. It is called *Loma-Si* and brings to the non-Indians' attention the needs of native Americans.)

For the suffering that came to Corrie and her family during World War II, the people of Israel honored her. The ceremony took place at Yad Vashem, a memorial to the Holocaust, which is situated outside the walls of the city of Jerusalem, set high on a hill. Visitors entering the museum there are met with the most horrifying pictures of the defenseless victims of the Nazis. The six million Jews, who were systematically massacred, are remembered in this place. One leaves—never to be the same again.

In the building adjoining the museum, an eternal flame burns in sacred memory of these persecuted people. It is inscribed Do NOT FORGET. The floor, a mosaic made up of small stones, each one representing a person killed, is inlaid with names that live on in history as being the most diabolical the world has ever known—the names of the death camps: Belsen, Auschwitz, Dachau, Buchenwald, and so forth, and then one reads *Ravensbruck*—the camp which held the ten Boom sisters. Ashes from bodies found in the death camps are buried under each concentration camp's name.

As people stand there, unashamedly they cry, remembering the "Betsies" who died in these concentration camps and the "Corries" who suffered the indignities, the deprivation, and loss of loved ones.

This memorial would give no hope, just a reminder of the most infamous event in history—until, as a Christian, you look at the walls around you. They are built from stones brought from the Sea of Galilee and are a reminder of the Prince of Peace, who walked along its shores bringing His love and forgiveness to all who would listen. This is the same Jesus who sustained Corrie in her darkest hours.

As the visitor leaves the memorial, a beautiful scene meets the eye—"The Avenue of Righteous Gentiles." It is a grove of olive trees and at the base of each tree is a plaque, bearing the name of a Gentile who helped the Jews in World War II. There in this beautiful, peaceful setting is a plaque which reads THE TEN BOOM FAMILY—one of the highest tributes the Israeli Government could pay these courageous people. Since 1844 in the little house in Haarlem, they had prayed constantly for the peace of Jerusalem and willingly suffered for its people.

Corrie was there the day the ten Boom tree was dedicated, February 28, 1968, exactly twenty-four years to the day the family was arrested.

Corrie remembered the dedication ceremony: "My thoughts turned away from the people who had been killed, to the ones who had been saved, because God used my family, friends, and me. I heard my father's voice say, 'If I die in prison, it will be an honor to have given my life for God's ancient people . . .'

" 'Father, Betsie, Willem, Kik—you gave your lives for God's chosen people,' I whispered."

Corrie spoke that day to the Jewish people gathered around her. Here is a part of what she said:

> I remember my sister Nollie telling me: "We love the Jews because we can thank them for the two greatest treasures: first of all, a book written by Jews. It is the Bible and we must thank Israel for it. It is a book which is almost bursting with good news and glorious promises. . . ."
>
> I want to thank you, the Jews, for this book. For the Bible has shown me the way to the second blessing which Nollie mentioned. It got me acquainted with my greatest Friend. He was a Jew. And this Friend is my Savior!
>
> . . . What a joy that in this book we see God's side of the history of the world. Many of you are expecting the Messiah to come, and so are we Christians. We believe He is coming again and He will do what He promised: "I will make all things new" [see Revelation 21:5].

The certificate from
the Queen, proclaiming
Corrie a Knight.

Corrie at the Palace with
Queen Wilhelmina, watching
a children's parade, 1960.

Corrie, seated at the family table in
the Beje, remembers the happy
family times. Papa and Mama ten
Boom's photo hangs on the wall.

Corrie shows where the Jews had to crawl into the hiding place.
Opening in wall makes it possible for visitors to the Beje to look
inside the hiding place.

The Beje today.

Tom Claus presents Corrie with plaque, indicating she is a member of the Indian tribes.

Corrie with her arm around elderly Indian woman.

At Yad Vashem, Israel, Corrie turns a handle to make the eternal flame burn brighter.

The ten Boom tree, planted in Israel by the government, to honor the bravery of Corrie and her family in saving Jewish lives.

The tree today.

10

Spreading Out Her Roots

Corrie working on one of her many books.

When Corrie was twelve, she decided she wanted to be a writer, and her vivid imagination conjured up a wonderful story about her sisters and cousins on holiday without their parents. She just knew she would be famous when the book was published! But Betsie, who had always been one to encourage her, now shattered her dreams. She told Corrie she was foolish for wanting to write a book. So the little girl decided she would not show her book to *anyone* and hid it in the attic of the Beje. Later, when she went up there to look at her precious manuscript, she found that nine-tenths of it had been eaten by mice! She was so upset she vowed she would *never* write again.

How thankful the readers of Corrie's inspiring books can be that she did not stick to that vow, but instead responded to the Lord's direction to write the many books that have blessed people all over the world.

Mimi Kyzer, who was with Corrie in Ravensbruck, is one who shares that feeling.

> It is marvelous how Corrie's books have been used by the Lord in so many countries. I know a little peasant woman in Switzerland. She is very poor: one room, one pan, one fork. *She* has read Corrie's books. God has given Corrie a great gift. She has great compassion and can bring the truth to very simple people. It makes a great impression on them. She says it like a child and everyone can understand.
>
> Even the shepherds in the Swiss Alps have read Corrie's books!

Her books, just like the Gospel, cut through all social barriers. Her writings bring the assurance of God's love and forgiveness, a promise of new beginnings.

After Corrie was released from Ravensbruck, she found that she was still waking up at three o'clock every morning for the dreaded roll call. She made valuable use of this time, because she began to put down all her experiences on paper. Others might toss and turn, exasperated that they could not sleep. But together with her Lord, Corrie was able to use the long night hours to glorify Him.

Her first book, the moving *A Prisoner and Yet*, published by Christian Literature Crusade, introduced Corrie to the Christian world and fast became a best-seller. The war was still fresh in the minds of people, and to hear from one who had suffered at the hands of the Nazis made compelling reading. Her pen was prolific, and obviously God had given her a gift of communication. Her travels with Brother Andrew led him to tell John and Elizabeth Sherrill, who had written his powerful story, *God's Smuggler*, to consider writing Corrie's amazing story. This brought about the dynamic co-authoring, with Corrie, of *The Hiding Place*.

Bill Barbour, president of the Fleming H. Revell Company, who arranged with Chosen Books to publish this great Christian classic, recalls:

> The Lord brought us all together to publish this tremendous story. To date, *The Hiding Place* has sold millions of copies.
>
> Through her books, Corrie has a global ministry. Over eight

million copies of her nineteen titles have been sold worldwide!

Eight million copies of books sold from the pen of that little girl who long ago vowed she would never write again!

Ernie Owen, the editorial director at Revell Company, remembers the first time he met Corrie:

> It was in a little French restaurant in New York City at our Revell sales conference. Our spirits had been lifted and our hearts warmed by reading the manuscript of *The Hiding Place*, and now at last we had the exciting opportunity of meeting the author personally.
>
> Corrie spoke to us that day about the love of Jesus, and the unspeakable joy and victory we have by surrendering our lives to Him. Not one person within the sound of her voice left the room that afternoon without the feeling that God had spoken the truth through her.

The Hiding Place was made into a film that changed the entire ministry of Christian films. It reached out into the secular world, showing that there was an audience who would respond to the Christian message in the market of the movie theatre.

Ruth Graham, who first brought *The Hiding Place* to the attention of World Wide Pictures, feeling it would make a tremendous motion picture, tells of her meeting Corrie:

> In 1960 my husband, Bill, and I were visiting in Switzerland. There I met Tante Corrie and her nephew Peter. That summer I first heard her story, and the greatest impression when I met her was *God brought her through all that, with a twinkle in her eyes!* She truly is one of God's merry saints!
>
> When I first read the manuscript of *The Hiding Place*, I knew that here was a story that had to be told on the screen. I didn't know anyone who had suffered so intensely for the Lord and for His people as Corrie had—and come through with absolutely nothing but love in her heart, even for her captors. Everywhere she has gone she has left the imprint of the Lord's love and gladness.
>
> As Corrie says, "When Christ is in the heart, the worst can happen but the best remains. And the best is yet to be!"

It is a miracle that the movie was ever made! The budget had been drawn up—$1.5 million—a small amount, compared to the average Hollywood production, but astronomical for a Christian film.

It was during the recession of 1973 that the funds were needed, and after much deliberation by the World Wide Pictures board, Billy Graham announced to a group meeting in Marco Island, Florida, that the film was being canceled. Corrie was in the audience. At first she was devastated, learning the news, but recovering quickly, she said to the small group around her, "Our Heavenly Father 'owns the cattle on a thousand hills.' We'll have to ask Him to sell a cow."

Then the miracle came—in the form of two people three thousand miles away in Orange County, California. Thelma and Edgar Elfstrom had, thirteen years before, suffered the tragic loss of their lovely nineteen-year-old daughter, Brenda Lynn. Years before, a trust fund of over fifty thousand dollars had been established for her.

Unaware of Billy Graham's announcement, the Elfstroms, that same day, placed a telephone call to Corrie's hotel room in Florida.

Edgar spoke, "Corrie, Thelma and I have been praying here and we feel the Lord wants us to give Brenda Lynn's trust fund toward the film."

Corrie's reaction: "Praise the Lord! He sold a cow!"

Plans for the film were immediately reinstated, but there was still a long way to go financially. The Lord showed Bill Brown, president of World Wide Pictures and executive producer of the film, a plan for developing a "Hiding Place Family." In a month's time there were forty-four thousand "family members" who pledged to pray and give towards the film on a monthly basis. Those people financed the film before it was ever finished!

Jimmy Collier, who directed *The Hiding Place* so sensitively and brought to each scene such a feeling of authenticity, established a deep rapport with Corrie. Together they would talk for hours about her life, her family, and her suffering. Through this came the framework that brought about the realism of the movie. Jimmy Collier reflected on his times with Corrie:

> Creating any film is a perilous journey. Relationships are quickly
> tested under the day-by-day pressures of production. Corrie and I

have managed four films together . . . quite illogical from any human perspective. This lady and I are separated by a century and several lifetimes, yet the communication and trust grew with each project.

Corrie is blessed with an active imagination, which the years have not diminished. It is perhaps her least-understood gift and it bound us together from the start. A part of Corrie will always be a child on a bicycle, bumping breathlessly over Haarlem's cobblestoned lanes. It helped her push back the gray walls and grim realities of Ravensbruck. It brought her laughter during the bitter post-war years, when laughter was thin. It has allowed her to sense the heart needs of untold thousands over the world.

It is a wonder of God when people enter our lives to enrich us. This daughter of Casper ten Boom continues to teach me . . . .

Allan Sloan, the celebrated writer who has won Emmys for several of his television scripts, co-wrote the screenplay of *The Hiding Place* with Larry Holben. Larry, a young writer of great talent, went to Holland to help with the publicity and any additional dialogue needed. He recalled the experience of meeting and working with Corrie ten Boom.

As I write this, I look up at a photograph of Corrie ten Boom on my wall. She sits, wrapped in a gray fur collar, hand to her face, in no way taken in by all the fuss of a film being made.

It was from Corrie and Betsie that I first learned that we find Christ most perfectly in the dark, painful places of human need. Corrie planted a seed of vision of discipleship that recognizes the incarnation and the cross as the great parables of our life in Him. As I look at the photograph on the wall, I see so clearly in her the spirit that shines from her face, the reality of resurrection hope, which is the promise we embrace in taking up the way of the cross.

As a Roman Catholic, I am encouraged by my faith to see the living presence of Jesus in those of His saints who follow Him faithfully. I doubt that I shall ever see that loving reality with more clarity than I have been privileged to see it in Corrie ten Boom.

The search to find someone to play Corrie was one that was conducted with a tremendous amount of prayer. She would have to be an outstanding actress—also one who could understand the spiritual dimension of the part. God found the perfect actress in Jeannette Clift, who excels in both categories. Jeannette speaks of this tremendous opportunity:

> I met Corrie for the first time at Jimmy Collier's house on the night that I had been told I was to play her in the movie. I looked at Corrie, this beautiful lady, and I thought, *Those are the bluest-blue eyes these brown eyes have ever looked into!*
>
> While we were filming, many times Corrie and I would be talking before a scene would start. They would call me on to the set and I would say, "Corrie, I am going to work now," and she would say, "You work; I pray."
>
> Corrie was very supportive and loving and she offered to me what Betsie offered to her: an illustration of God's power through a life yielded to Him. Because of her, I am stronger. Because of Him, we rejoice in eternal fellowship. I thank the Lord for all that He has given us of His joy, absolute joy. We see it in Corrie—JOY!

The role of Betsie was also one which humanly would be difficult to cast. But again God had the perfect person in Julie Harris, herself a gentle, loving soul, who is particularly sensitive to those who suffer. Her portrayal of Betsie was one that would always stand out in her career as being a deeply satisfying role. Julie Harris tells of the experience:

> Bill Brown of World Wide Pictures sent me a copy of *The Hiding Place*. He and the film's director, James Collier, were thinking of me to play Betsie. I read the book in one sitting and loved it and, oh, how thrilled I was to think of the possibility of playing the part of Betsie.
>
> Then in February 1974 my dream came true, and I was stepping on a plane at Kennedy International Airport with Jeannette Clift, who was to play Corrie. We were taking off for Europe.
>
> The picture was finished in June. I was sad to think it was over—but really happy that I was part of it . . . As I look back on those precious months working on *The Hiding Place*, I saw firsthand the miracle of love through Jesus Christ our Lord.

Later Julie wrote to Corrie:

> I find strength that comes from loving Christ and I do believe with all
> my heart He is our Hiding Place. Corrie, you brought me closer to
> Jesus. I will always hear you say, "Jesus is Victor!" I love you very
> much.

Equally important was the casting of Papa ten Boom. Veteran actor
Arthur O'Connell, who portrayed him so convincingly, has said:

> Usually when I finish a picture, it's out of sight—out of mind. But
> that is not so with *The Hiding Place.* I am reminded every day of Papa
> ten Boom and his children . . . real people, whose actions and mo-
> tives were Christlike . . . and I try to emulate them. I think about
> the Lord more often and my relationship with Him now is so much
> closer.

At one of the film production meetings in Haarlem, there were two
people present who had lived at the Beje during the war. Hans Poley,
who had helped Corrie in her underground work, and Eusie, who had
now become a rabbi. Their presence added tremendously to the atmosphere from which the director and cast could gather valuable information.

Eusie sang in Hebrew a song in a voice that throbbed with all the
passion that comes from the heartbreak his people have endured over
the centuries. He closed with the benediction from Numbers 6:24-
26 KJV:

> The Lord bless thee, and keep thee: The Lord make
> his face shine upon thee, and be gracious unto thee:
> The Lord lift up his countenance upon thee, and give
> thee peace.

It was March 1974 that the filming began and the weather was freezing. Many difficulties beset the company, but Frank Jacobson, the producer, says it was Corrie who showed that all these things could be
surmounted. He remembers that first day before the cameras rolled:

In her quiet way, Corrie lifted her hands as unto the Lord and asked for His blessing and guidance. It was a very solemn moment, as it was just as if Corrie were speaking audibly face-to-face with the Lord. Several days after the filming began, we experienced attacks of demonic proportions. Again, with arms outstretched, Corrie had a personal conversation with the Lord. After prayer she said, "Frank, Satan always does this kind of thing, but do not worry. I will continue to uphold each of you."

During those trying times, we worked with faith, secure in the Lord, as Corrie, with Ellen de Kroon, spent hours in continuous prayer to the Lord.

Frank Jacobson's wife, Dorothy, and daughter Chris accompanied him during the filming. Each morning they would meet with Corrie for prayer for fifteen or twenty minutes and read from the Word. Dorothy says:

> I was impressed with the amount of work that she accomplished each day, and with such apparent lack of weariness, for one her age. I realized that Corrie leaned on the Lord for her strength and for the answers to the day's problems and decisions.
>
> She asked His help in every situation that would save her strength. One day we were driving into Haarlem, which was very crowded. As we neared the Grote Markt, Corrie started praying for a parking place, so she would not have far to walk. No sooner had she finished the prayer, than a man backed out of a perfect spot. We were, as Corrie says, "Nestling instead of wrestling!"
>
> She showed us that we can expect God to help in every situation, large or small. We learned so much from her.

Corrie enjoyed the many amusing things that happened during the making of the film. Bill Brown enjoys telling this story:

> Corrie was not quite so well known in England as in America, and when we were filming, a reporter asked me, "Tell me, what were the names of Corrie's *nine* sisters?" When I said there were only three sisters, the reporter looked puzzled and said, "But your news release said the ten Boom sisters lived upstairs over the watchshop!"

Bill Brown speaks of Corrie as being a beautiful blend of the human and spiritual:

A perfect combination of Martha and Mary. So down to earth, concerned about everyone around her . . . yet with a constant and complete trust in her Savior.

For Corrie it was a time of having to live again the most heartbreaking experiences in her life. As she walked through Haarlem and saw the Germans once more "invading" the streets—only this time in the guise of actors—the old feelings of dread returned to her. But particularly difficult for her was to see her family recreated. Corrie reflects: "Sometimes it was hard for me to relive the difficult life during the war. To see Father suffer again, played by Arthur O'Connell, who is so much like my real father, moved my heart. When we were filming in Haarlem, a man came up to me and said, 'I have loved your father so much and now I saw him walking in the street!' This man had tears in his eyes. This was the reaction I had when I first saw Arthur dressed as Papa.

"Then when I first saw Julie Harris playing Betsie, she was so moving. She herself is so much like my sister. Just in portraying her I felt Julie must have suffered deeply.

"It was a little funny for me when I saw Jeannette Clift playing *me!* But then I quickly got used to her playing the part; it was not a show; it was just as if she were really living it.

"Sometimes it was very difficult, as it showed the happy family life I enjoyed many years ago—it made me very homesick. Then came the time of the arrest and imprisonment, and I had to relive it all again. It was not easy. I had to say, 'Lord, I cannot go through this again . . . to see my family suffer . . . .' The reality was not less than I remembered.

"Then I got an encouraging answer from the Lord: 'It was the start of your suffering, but now you can see it was the start of work in My kingdom, because now I have used you in your talks, in books, and in the movie to bring the Gospel to many, many people,' and in that moment I had to thank the Lord. *Hallelujah!*

"Isn't it a joy to think the Lord can use all these experiences to show that whatever happens to you in life, when you are a child of God, the best remains!"

The premiere of *The Hiding Place* was scheduled for September 1975. In a beautiful theater in Beverly Hills, California, an audience of thirteen hundred, comprised of many well-known stars of Hollywood, gathered to see this motion picture that would touch so many lives. As the last person was seated and the house lights dimmed, an exit door opened and a tear-gas bomb was thrown inside. The theater had to be evacuated, but remarkably there was no panic, as the audience streamed out into the busy street—eyes red from the stinging fumes. The fire department found the bomb and on its side was the emblem of the swastika. The conclusion was drawn that the bomb was thrown by a member of the American Nazi Party to demonstrate their hatred for this film and all it portrayed.

At first it seemed the evening would be a disaster, but the Lord used it in a remarkable way. The busy street was turned into a place of worship as Pat Boone, Cliff Barrows, Billy Graham, and Corrie conducted a service. The audience sang hymns and prayed. Those passing by were amazed to see this extremely well-dressed, large crowd participating in a street meeting!

The publicity went around the world. In many countries the newspapers carried the story and a picture on their front pages. Satan had given thousands of dollars worth of free publicity!

Scores of rave reviews began to appear from such sophisticated reviewers as Rex Reed, who gave it his top four-star rating. In *Vogue* magazine he wrote:

> . . . *The Hiding Place* is one those rare, magical films touched with the sincerity and sweetness of human goodness. It's a long, involving tapestry of faith and strength in the face of brutality and injustice that moved me deeply. It's the kind of meaningful film that is almost never financed by Hollywood studios . . . .

Reed, who writes for the *New York Daily News* and other newspapers throughout the USA, also wrote:

> *The Hiding Place*, like the valiant ten Booms who lived it, seems divinely inspired. Every man, woman and child with a Christian heart should consider it an honor to see it . . . The film is a hymn to the kind of galvanizing inner perseverance that kept them from going mad . . . .
>
> What a genuine pleasure to see a movie about the affirmation of life instead of the denigration of life . . . .

Because 15 million people have been reached through *The Hiding Place*, not only in America, but in Indonesia, Australia, France, Greece, and so many other countries, some of the "whys" that arose in Corrie's heart when she found herself in the darkness of Ravensbruck have been answered. Her nephew Peter van Woerden, now an evangelist in Switzerland, remembers the day he, too, asked God, "Why?"

> I will never forget that day in 1944 when my mother [Nollie] entered my room, sobbing her heart out—I had never heard her in such a state of despair before. "Peter," she stammered, "news has just come that both Corrie and Betsie have been transferred to a concentration camp in Germany. Already Father died a prisoner, and now I will also lose my two sisters! I'm afraid I will not be able to take it . . ."
>
> I was speechless. What could I say to comfort Mama? It seemed that everything had gone wrong since that fateful day in February, when the Gestapo had clamped down on the hiding place for Jews in the Barteljorisstraat.
>
> Many question marks filled my heart when mother left my room. I fell on my knees and pleaded, "Lord give me *Your* light on what is happening. Why all this? What will be the outcome? God, did You forget us?"
>
> I opened my Bible. Its pages fell open in the Book of Jeremiah. The passage which caught my attention was this one:
>
>> Blessed is the man that trusteth in the Lord, and whose hope the Lord is. For he shall be as a tree planted by the waters, and that spreadeth out her roots by the river, and shall not see when heat cometh, but her leaf shall be green; and shall not be careful in the year of drought, neither shall cease from yielding fruit.
>>
>> Jeremiah 17:7, 8KJV
>
> Oh, what comfort this word brought to my heart! With the open Bible in my hand, I ran downstairs. "Mama, here is a word from God for us. Look, is it not wonderful?" It was a definite promise from the Lord, which lighted our darkness that day and caused us to wipe away our tears, knowing that all was under control.

Grandfather's tree has not ceased to bear fruit. Aunt Corrie's and Aunt Betsie's experiences of Christ's victory in the hell of Ravensbruck opened the way for lasting monuments to God's faithfulness to be erected through literature and film. Untold blessings are pouring forth to touch millions. God is faithful to His Word!

And—by the way—*Boom* is the Dutch word for *tree!*

Betsie's vision of traveling the world with Corrie has come true. Peter wrote to his Tante Corrie after seeing the premiere of *The Hiding Place* in Germany:

I thought, *Through the film, Corrie and Betsie are both going around the world with the message that the Lord gave them, even as Tante Betsie saw it.* Isn't it wonderful?

John and Elizabeth Sherrill,
who coauthored
The Hiding Place with Corrie.

**Bill Barbour of Fleming H. Revell Company
presents Corrie with a copy of *Each New Day*.**

**With Edgar and Thelma Elfstrom,
whom the Lord used to help make
THE HIDING PLACE film possible.**

**Ruth Graham with Corrie, discussing the possibility
of *The Hiding Place* book becoming a movie.**

Corrie, as Larry Holben stated, "...in no way taken in by all the fuss of filming."

As research for the film, Frank Jacobson, the producer, and Corrie visit a concentration camp. It was hard for her to relive those dark days.

Corrie meets Jeannette Clift, who portrayed her, on the first day of filming in Haarlem.

Corrie speaking to the cast and crew on the first day of filming.

Production meeting in Holland.

A wonderful rapport existed between Jimmy Collier and Corrie, while filming in Holland.

Julie Harris, who portrayed Betsie, sharing happy moments with Corrie.

Arthur O'Connell as Papa.

Filming in the Grote Markt.

Julie Harris as Betsie and David Shepherd as "Eusie."

Frank Jacobson, the film's producer, with Corrie and Bill Brown, the executive producer.

Corrie with some of the actresses who played women from "Hut 28" — Corrie's barracks at Ravensbruck.

On a visit to Haarlem during filming, Billy Graham and George Wilson are shown the watch shop by Corrie.

Billy Graham with Julie Harris, Arthur O'Connell, Jeannette Clift, and Corrie.

From out of the window of the watch shop, Corrie watches the filming.

The premiere of THE HIDING PLACE in Beverly Hills.

Julie Harris is interviewed by Pat Boone for television cameras outside the theater.

Roy Rogers and Dale Evans Rogers attend.

Billy Graham with Corrie and Jeannette Clift.

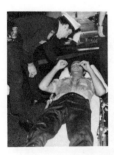

Fireman overcome by fumes from smoke bomb tossed into the theater at the premiere.

Checking the theater later for evidence.

Beverly Hills' largest street meeting ever!

11
Shalom!

Outside "Shalom."

In her travels in sixty-three countries, Corrie has slept in thousands of beds—some in the sumptuous homes of millionaires, but often in the humblest of dwellings—in the remotest parts of Africa—in the war zone of Vietnam.

But God did not forget the desire of Corrie's heart as she prayed to Him, while the train took her from the hell of Ravensbruck to freedom in Holland: . . . *a nice home, Lord, with good food, music,* and *the company of others.*

On February 28, 1944, she had been taken to prison. Thirty-three years later, on February 28, 1977, at the age of eighty-four, she stepped across the threshold of the home God had provided for His child in California. Here would be peace. Corrie named the house *Shalom!*

With Corrie came Pamela Rosewell, who had traveled with her since Ellen de Kroon married. Officially a secretary/companion, Pamela is so much more. This gentle, loving girl has also become a member of Corrie's "family." Corrie says, "My constant companion and co-worker is Pam Rosewell, who has worked with me since 1976. Pam comes from England; we are a happy team. She works side by side with me and is young and able. I needed her before as a fellow tramp, but I need her help now more than ever as a teammate."

Together they made the house into a home. Corrie was like a little girl who had been granted her fondest wish. She unpacked and slept in her very own bed! She was able to wear clothes that were too bulky to pack in her suitcase. A magnificent mandarin gown that had been given to her years before came out of storage. Her favorite books ("even a big concordance!") could be placed on shelves easily accessible to her. Photographs of the family graced the living room, and Papa's striking portrait looked down on his daughter Corrie. A photograph of Saint Bavo's commanded a special place too.

She said: "I have never been as happy as this since I lived in the Beje."

Then there was the joy of being able to listen to her favorite classical music. The strains of Bach filled the house, as Corrie played the organ in praise to her Lord, remembering His goodness and faithfulness to her.

Now she could entertain her friends—pouring a cup of tea gave Corrie such joy. Her guests were joyous too, watching Corrie's radiant face. Outside in her beautiful garden, she planted flowers and was able to watch and feed the birds, which have always brought her such delight.

When Corrie first entered the doors of Shalom, she dedicated it to her Lord. He promised her that she would reach more people than ever before with the Gospel. Here she counseled personally and by telephone hundreds of people. She began writing more books—sometimes three at a time! Movies were made from the house and her garden, which reached out to so many. Letters poured in from all over the world from people needing Corrie's spiritual help.

Corrie was now near to the offices of "Christians Incorporated," her official ministry. From there is sent the magazine called *The Hiding Place*, a beautifully illustrated presentation, filled with news of Corrie and her outreach for the Lord.

The late Walter Gastil played an important part in Corrie's ministry, and she turned to him so many times for wisdom and guidance. He and his wife, Maud, were close friends of hers, and when he died, Corrie felt a tremendous loss.

In charge of this ministry today are a dedicated couple, Bill and Bettie Butler. Bettie, looking back, remembers her first encounter with Corrie:

> I was taking Corrie and several ladies from one church to another, where she was the noon speaker. We had just gone two blocks in the car, when I realized that I had missed my turn. Corrie had already noticed this fact and announced it out loud (with slight irritation!). I assured her that we would be there right on time. But I added, "Pray for me." No sooner were the words out of my mouth when Corrie *did* pray out loud for me. It is a trait that endeared her to me then and has ever since. Never does one have to wait for prayer, when they give Corrie a request.
>
> We didn't realize it then, but we were soon to form a close relationship as teammates. A group of us met with Corrie four or five times, ironing out business details and determining how Corrie's work would best be handled. Corrie's confidence that the Holy Spirit would guide us in this new responsibility of overseeing her work was very evident when she turned to my husband, Bill, and said, "I trust you." Those three words settled our relationship. They were like a warm blanket enfolding us. It was a trust that was very humbling, and we take it very seriously.

It has become more and more difficult for Corrie and Pam to answer all the mail that pours into Shalom and the offices of Christians Incorporated. Bettie Butler helps answer mail on Corrie's behalf, and sometimes they have sat in the garden going over the precious greetings and requests that have come. This has brought Corrie such joy: scribbled messages on marvelous pictures from imaginative children; letters in shaky handwriting from some in their nineties are part of the tremendous volume of mail. Corrie has delighted in receiving pictures of adorable babies and pretty little girls, all named *Corrie!*

Bettie Butler goes on to say, "Of course the most treasured responses are when someone writes back that he has been released from some dreadful bondage as a result of hearing from Corrie. And, more importantly, when someone writes that he has accepted Jesus Christ. There is much to rejoice over! Through my close and unique association with Corrie, I have grown in my faith as I have observed firsthand her childlike trust in the Lord."

Bill Butler tells of the blessing that comes with working with Corrie:

My close relationship to Corrie began in 1973. Since then an unusual relationship of both trust and love has developed. Always we feel as one on matters concerning her ministry. Her top priority is always getting out the Good News along with a high interest in the support of missionaries around the world. God made funds available for this work through Corrie's book sales. Not only that, but she is financing the publication of many of her books in Eastern European languages.

I have many personal memories stored away. One delightful event took place while Corrie was filming the Indian movie *Loma-si* in Arizona. Everyone celebrated her birthday with a beautiful cake, brought by her Indian friends. That evening she told us story after story. One of them was about the day she was born. Her mother recorded in her diary, *This day I was delivered of a sickly little blue baby that we've named Corrie . . . I don't believe she'll last long.* An uncle added his thoughts in the diary, *It would be best if she were taken quickly.* We all laughed with Corrie, as she related this, and we realized that here she was many years later, spending long days filming (which is very tiring) and celebrating her eighty-sixth birthday!

The most inspiring aspect of Corrie is her faith, always evident, never wavering. One of her favorite ways to end a letter is to state, "Jesus is Victor." This statement shall always represent Corrie to me and to those of us who have had the high privilege of serving with and for this wonderful servant of the Lord.

"I was in prison and you visited me."
See Matthew 25:36

The work that is nearest to Corrie's heart is her prison ministry. With James F. Collier directing, Corrie made an incredibly effective movie called *The One Way Door*. Jimmy recalls:

> Corrie's "prison film" grew out of a series of backyard conversations,
> in which I hurled questions at her—at times, brutal questions. I was
> attempting to voice the unspoken hostility and pain that this captive
> audience would feel at the audacity of a "double-old grandmother"
> daring to address them. Corrie instantly picked up on the "game." A
> thin, majestic smile formed on the beautifully landscaped face and
> she fired back, "I may be your oldest teammate, but I know what it
> means to live behind a door that only opens from the outside." In
> that moment she gave me the opening line of the film.

The One Way Door is shown all over the world in jails and prisons
with amazing results. Hardened prisoners come to see it, perhaps ex-
pecting to jeer, but sit transfixed as this amazing lady looks right at them
from the screen and says:

> Do you know what it is like to spend four months in solitary con-
> finement?

The acts of pretense are swept away by her direct, loving presence
on the screen. The prisoners see that here is someone who really knows
what it is to suffer and who *cares*.

When she was a young girl, Corrie's father asked her to visit some
women in prison. Papa worked among the prisoners, but Corrie told
him she could not—she was too scared to go near a prison. Corrie recalled: "When I passed a prison, I always turned my eyes in the other
direction. I was afraid. Later, when I was in solitary confinement for four
months, alone, then I remembered what I had said to Father. I asked
forgiveness in Jesus' name. I was so lonesome.

"In a letter written from prison, I wrote, 'How greatly a prison
deprives people of the most elementary conditions of life! If God still
grants me chances, I hope to work in the area of rehabilitation. I will
now also dare to visit a prison cell, which I did not do before.'"

The Lord *did* give Corrie another chance, and today many prisoners
find consolation through her ministry and have been led to give their
lonely, broken lives to Jesus Christ.

Corrie said: "Some time ago I had heart trouble and had to choose between going to heaven or having a 'pacemaker.' Although my longing was be in heaven, the Lord made it clear that there was still work for me to do here. Coming from the operating room, I asked the Lord why He had given me back my life. His answer was very clear: 'There is an important work to do. Bring people who work in prisons together and train volunteers to work in prisons and jails, particularly in those places where the Gospel is not being brought.'

"As a result of this vision, the Association of Christian Prison Workers came into being, with Duane Pederson as its first president."

Hanging on one of the walls of Shalom is a plaque made by some of the inmates of San Quentin which reads:

CORRIE TEN BOOM—PRISONER OF THE LORD.

It was to this grim fortress of San Quentin that Corrie went with Duane Pederson to minister to the men behind its foreboding walls on September 25, 1977. This would be one of her last public-speaking engagements. (Now eighty-six years old, she knew she had to choose between staying at home and being able to write more books, make movies, oversee her prison ministry, and support her missionary programs, or continue to travel. The Lord showed her very clearly that her ministry would be from the house He had given her.)

As she waited outside the gates of San Quentin, a young girl who was lining up with the prisoners' wives, mothers, and girl friends recognized Corrie. In a stage whisper she turned to her friends and said, "That's Corrie ten Boom!" Then she ran over, wanting to hug Corrie. The girl was bedraggled and pitiful to look at, and Corrie (in her Dutch way) had never been one to want to hug people. But now it was Corrie who reached out and hugged this girl. It was a very touching moment.

Duane Pederson was present at this scene. He was to take Corrie into the prison and escort her to the chapel. Duane recalled the scene outside San Quentin:

It affected me deeply. Corrie, as she came back after hugging that girl, said to me, "So often it is the wives and families who hurt the most." I suddenly saw a whole new perspective—another side, not only of Corrie, but of the prison ministry—that there is a ministry that needs to be conducted amongst the *families*. There are parents who are suffering, the wives, and the girl friends of those behind bars.

That day the men listened intently to Corrie and many made decisions for Christ. It was the fact that she had come through her life and been able to surmount it and no longer be bitter.

It is almost impossible for me to find words to express all that this incredible woman has meant to my life. It has to do with the giving up of self—with being willing to give the kind of commitment which a fifty-three-year-old lady would make—then to travel for thirty-three years around the world, without a home. Corrie has helped me to see my commitment in better perspective and this by her life example.

Chaplain Harry Howard, who together with his wife, Elva (Kay), ministers to the prisoners of San Quentin in such a remarkable way, remembers the effect that Corrie had on his young life:

In 1949 I was leading a meeting as president of the Intervarsity Christian Leadership, on the campus of the University of Idaho at Moscow, Idaho. Even though I was a Christian and leading the group, the idea of going into full-time ministry was far from what I wanted to do.

Corrie spoke, and as I became aware of how much she had given for Christ, I asked what I had given. Along with others, Corrie was influential in my going into the ministry.

When Corrie came to speak at San Quentin, so many years later, it was a deeply emotional day for me. My parents were also present, and it was my wedding anniversary. Four men were baptized that day, and one became a staunch deacon. He was paroled later to Teen Challenge in San Francisco and has led a dedicated life in Christ ever since.

The young man to whom Chaplain Howard referred is Dennis Whitman. Here, in Dennis's own words, he tells of the way Corrie touched his life.

I first heard about Corrie ten Boom while I was doing time in San Quentin. I had been a Christian about four months, when I started hearing about a Christian named Corrie. She had done time in a German concentration camp and I heard how she kept her faith while in the camp.

About a week before she came to San Quentin, our Chaplain, Harry Howard, showed us the movie *The Hiding Place.* It really had an impact on my life. It helped to really strengthen my faith in Christ—what faith in Him can do.

It just happened that the day Corrie came to Quentin was the day I was going to be baptized. What she had to say in our church service about her imprisonment, and what Christ taught her in the prison will probably continue to have an impact on my life, until I go to be with the Lord.

God used Corrie at a crucial time in my Christian life, and at that time only a testimony like Corrie's could have really reached me.

I thank God for Corrie, and God has put a love in my heart for this Christian lady.

Corrie has only cried a few times in her adult life. Once was at the Queen's speech on the radio, saying that Holland had surrendered to the Germans. Then when she heard that Papa died while a prisoner, Corrie wept her heart out, thinking of this gentle, good man who had always been so understanding and loving to her. Shortly after she was released from Ravensbruck, she heard Bach being played, and all the emotions that had been pent up inside her, poured out—the melody recalling days that would never come back again—the happy family life in the Beje. She cried again, when she sat in a private screening theatre to see for the first time her story *The Hiding Place* as a movie. The reality of the suffering, the scenes of Betsie and Papa made this brave Dutch woman experience once more the agony she had known.

Corrie came near to crying the day she went to San Quentin. She said: "As we were going inside that day, all of the feelings, the sound of the barred doors slamming behind me—all of the sounds of walking into that prison—brought me closer to crying than I had for a long time."

The unshed tears God used that day. Corrie's compassion was apparent to the prisoners. One wrote:

Your message that day touched me to the depth of my heart. I now know Jesus died for me on the cross, so I may live and be forgiven of my many sins. God works in many wonderful ways—He used you to reach me. I'm now reading the Bible every day and, as I search the

Word of God, it's all becoming easier for me to comprehend. I want
to thank you for remembering me in your prayers.

Corrie has used many illustrations in her talks in and out of prison
that have helped her audiences capture the powerful meaning of having
Jesus Christ in our lives. One is her example of the embroidery.

Holding up the wrong side of it, she will say: "Look at this piece of
embroidery. The wrong side is chaos. But look at the beautiful picture
on the other side—the right side!" Then she recites one of her favorite
poems:

My life is but a weaving, between my God and me,
I do not chose the colors, He worketh steadily.
Oftimes He weaveth sorrow, and I in foolish pride,
Forget He sees the upper, and I the underside.
Not 'til the loom is silent, and shuttles cease to fly,
Will God unroll the canvas and explain the reason why:
The dark threads are as needful in the skillful Weaver's hand,
As the threads of gold and silver in the pattern He has planned!

GRANT COLFAX TULLAR

Then Corrie concludes: "We now see the wrong side; God sees His
side all the time. One day we shall see the embroidery from His side and
thank Him for every answered and unanswered prayer."

Joni Eareckson was paralyzed in a swimming accident. Her shining
faith looks beyond the chaos of the wrong side of the embroidery, too, to
see God's perfect plan for her life. She knows what it is like to feel
imprisoned. Joni tells of how Corrie helped her overcome one of her
greatest fears:

I first met Corrie ten Boom through reading *The Hiding Place*. It was
three years after I got out of the hospital, and I immediately felt a
kind of kinship with her, because she had suffered confinement for
quite a long time. I was going through a time of confinement and was
battling that feeling of claustrophobia that everyone faces in a wheel-
chair.

When I saw *The Hiding Place* movie and the scene where Corrie
is in solitary confinement in a small cell with only a very small win-

dow, it had a deep effect on me. Just to see a prison always does something to me. Recently I visited one in Virginia, and to go through those doors with the bars that are locked behind you associates with me the feeling that "you can't move—you can't go anywhere—you don't have freedom!"

When I was in the hospital, there was a room that had a window with a tree outside. When I saw the leaves move in the wind, I was jealous of them, because I thought they were so much more mobile than I and enjoyed so much more freedom. I felt I was worth less than a leaf.

One night I was watching the film *The Birdman of Alcatraz* on television, and right at the beginning where the warden tells Robert Stroud, "You are going to have to remain in solitary for the rest of your life!"—I panicked. I just started crying, because of the overwhelming feeling of claustrophobia. It struck me when I saw the look on his face. It was the same terror I had known so many times.

I had the same impression when I saw Corrie's confinement. I felt a real identification with her, and all she lived through and went through in prison, and the claustrophobia she overcame. I saw the beautiful, the very free spirit of Christ in her that would not be confined behind those barbed-wire fences . . . .

We met at a Christian Booksellers Convention. I was there to introduce my first book, and she was there to introduce one of her many books!

Corrie was being escorted down a carpeted corridor . . . . We just met in the middle of the hall. For me, it was a very overwhelming experience—just to come face-to-face with her. I was so honored and surprised that she knew who I was. She just reached for my hand—even though I could not offer it—and just like a grandmother might hold your hand, she patted the top of it. At first I thought this was unusual, because I was paralyzed, but she just reached right out without any hesitation. Since then I have learned that she has worked with so many handicapped people, so it was a very natural thing for her to do.

Then in her Dutch accent she said something very touching. "One day we will dance and sing together in heaven, when the Lord gives us new bodies!" I just felt like I was listening to a matriarch.

With Pamela Rosewell among the flowers in the garden.

Corrie in her very own bed!

Playing the organ in praise to God.

Listening to Bach on the stereo.

Working with Pamela on her correspondence.

Pouring tea for her guest, Doris Busby.

With photographer Russ Busby, who has taken so many photos of her.

Visitors to Shalom, Billie and Cliff Barrows.

Corrie shows her delight in working in the kitchen.

Caring for her flowers.

Filling one of her bird feeders.

With a longtime friend,
Brother Andrew.

Filming in the garden of Shalom with Jimmy Collier
and Cliff Barrows.

Welcoming Bill and Bettie Butler.

The late Walter Gastil,
whose friendship
meant so much to Corrie.

In her living room, with some of her books and Papa's portrait.

With Duane Pederson outside San Quentin State Prison.

Chaplain Harry Howard presenting Corrie with plaque made by prisoners at San Quentin.

Corrie demonstrates a lesson through embroidery. The underside represents our lives—chaos.

Corrie watches, as Dennis Whitman is baptized by prison chaplains.

The right side—
God's—beautiful!

12

"This Is *Your* Life, Corrie ten Boom"

Pamela Rosewell escorts Corrie onto the stage for the tribute to her, filmed in Denver.

In July 1978, during the Christian Booksellers Convention in Denver, Colorado, people flew in from around the world to take part in a tribute for Corrie ten Boom. Corrie had come to this city at the request of her publishing company, Fleming H. Revell Company, to help promote her new book *Each New Day*. Little did she know that they were planning, together with World Wide Pictures, a "This Is Your Life" type program called *Corrie: The Lives She's Touched*, to be filmed before an audience in Boettcher Hall.

The house lights dimmed and Cliff Barrows announced to the crowd of two thousand admirers: "Ladies and Gentlemen, I want you to welcome with me God's most wonderful vagabond, our tramp for the Lord, *Corrie ten Boom*."

The audience cheered and applauded as Corrie, escorted by Pam Rosewell, came onto the platform. How Corrie sparkled, as one by one people from out of her past came on to the stage to reminisce with her, and tell how she had affected their lives. It was deeply moving when, from the side of the stage, in semidarkness, Corrie heard a passage from Bach being played on the grand piano. The pianist was her greatly loved nephew Peter van Woerden, who had flown from Switzerland to be with his Tante Corrie on her special night. The two embraced and then remembered together the dark days when the family members were arrested, but then told of God's goodness to them through all their suffering.

There were people who had actually been in the Beje during the war—Hans and Mies Poley flew from Holland; Diet Erlich, who had been with Corrie in Vught; Truus Benes, the nurse who had given Corrie her first meal after being released; Lotte Reimeringer, who helped establish the rehabilitation center. Adding to the joy of the evening was special music by Evie Tornquist, the Bill Gaither Trio, George Beverly Shea, and Tedd Smith, who had composed the compelling, beautiful score for the sound track of *The Hiding Place*.

Others included Jeannette Clift, who had played Corrie so convincingly in the film; Joni Eareckson; Tom Claus, Pastor Do Van Nguyen, Ruth Graham (with a long-distance telephone call from Billy Graham, who could not be there); Bill Barbour of Revell Company and many, many more. Mary Crowley, president of Home Interiors, presented Corrie with a life-size portrait, which Mary had had commissioned—her way of saying *thank you* for all the joy Corrie had brought into her life.

Carole Carlson and Jamie Buckingham came to share their greetings, authors who had so sensitively co-authored with Corrie *In My Father's House* and *Tramp for the Lord*, respectively.

One of the guests that evening really embodied all those who Corrie has led to the Lord—Beth Brain, an airline stewardess with Northwestern Airlines. She told the audience that night what Corrie has meant to her:

I had grown up in a traditional church and, as a child, knew that God was a vital part of my life. But, as I grew older, I had so many searching questions about God and life.

I joined Northwestern, as it would be a chance to get away from home and be independent. But flying didn't really help—it only gave me more freedom to go astray. During vacation I began reading Peter and Catherine Marshall's books, and they touched something deep within me. The vacation passed, and I managed to catch an earlier flight than expected. I ran for the plane and was the last one on.

Across the aisle from me sat Corrie and Ellen—I did not know who they were, only that they must be celebrities by the crowd of people who kept coming up to them. During the flight, Ellen got in conversation with me and told me about *The Hiding Place* and The Living Bible. She said I could hear Corrie speak in Minneapolis.

When we landed, Ellen introduced me to Corrie and we went our separate ways. I bought *The Hiding Place* and *The Living Bible* and began to read. The next week, while on a flight from Rochester to Minneapolis, Ellen boarded the plane. Now that is a miracle—you almost never see the same passenger twice, unless they are commuters. At that point God really got my attention, and I went with my mother to hear Corrie speak.

I heard Corrie explain who Jesus was, and what He did, and that He is alive today. She said that He desires for each of us to ask Him into our lives to live in us. When Corrie presented the message in such a simple, childlike fashion, I understood and when she gave the opportunity to pray silently and ask Christ in, I did. It was the greatest decision I've ever made!

Corrie was God's instrument for touching my life, and from her I inherited an ability to see God in simple, everyday illustrations. Now I know that God was able to touch me, because my parents had entrusted me to Him when I was still an infant and over the years—especially the difficult ones—Mom continued to pray for me.

In a sense I follow in Corrie's footsteps. She has been a "tramp for the Lord," and now I am doing the same as I travel across the country.

I later learned that Corrie and Ellen were on the "wrong" flight the day we met. They had left Seattle a day early! God is so good! He really has everything under control.

Corrie and I have met a few times since then, and every time I have been blessed by her simple childlike faith. What an example her life is to me and to many. Her life directs us to Jesus.

The joy of the Lord had shone on Corrie's face throughout the program, but when Beth Brain gave her testimony, her radiance was even more apparent. Here was what the Lord had called Corrie to do—to win souls.

Cliff Barrows, who emceed the program so masterfully, told Corrie at the end of the program:

> Tante Corrie, there are so many others who wished they could have been here: The hundreds of Jews whose lives you saved through your work in the underground; those who found Christ in your meetings; the inmates of prisons around the world whom you have influenced and who have found a new freedom—a freedom, which only Christ can give. Then there are thousands of Christians who have been motivated and encouraged in their Christian walk and witness, through your example—countless lives that you have touched.
>
> But Tante Corrie, I remember what you told me three or four years ago. You were sitting in our home, talking one night, and you said, "You know I come to America and the halo gets so heavy on my head. You Americans say, 'Thank you Corrie, you preach so well;' or, 'Corrie, you are so wonderful,' and so on." Then you said you worried about it and prayed about it.

It *has* been hard for Corrie to accept all the adulation that has come to her, because she knows that all the glory is the Lord's. As she prayed about it, the Lord showed her a beautiful way of using the tributes and accolades: Each one would represent a beautiful flower, and then at night, she would collect them into a beautiful bouquet and give them back to Jesus, saying, "Here, Lord, they belong to You!"

That night in Denver, Cliff Barrows's lovely wife, Billie, presented Corrie with a beautiful bouquet of flowers. As the program came to an end, Corrie looked up to heaven and raised the bouquet to the Lord, her face shining with His radiance and love.

The tributes would always be for Him, the One who had died for her, the One who had walked each day with her through the valleys and the mountaintops of her life—the Lord Jesus Christ—the One who would be with His daughter through all Eternity.

He who knows the future allowed the tribute in Denver to be Corrie's last public appearance—only one month after it, she suffered a serious stroke. The Christian world was saddened to think of this vibrant, vigorous woman stilled by such a paralyzing illness. Corrie herself fought back with all of the old, indomitable spirit, and gradually—together with Pamela and Lotte, who had come from Holland to help take care of her—she worked to bring back the use of her hands and her speech.

The once-energetic woman would often have to sit still for many days at a time. But to those around her, she went on exuding the love of Christ. Her mother so many years before had suffered a stroke, and Corrie and her family knew that though she could not speak to them, she was still loving them and praying for them. History was repeating itself. Through Corrie's brilliant blue eyes one could still see Jesus. Someone once said, "The eyes are the windows of the soul" and Corrie's "windows" were clear and radiant, triumphant over the helplessness in which she now found herself.

Once a cloud passed over the radiant eyes, and Corrie did not feel the Lord was as close to her. Pamela telephoned Corrie's pastor, the Reverend Chuck Mylander, and he came to pray with her. Tears coursed down the cheeks of this beautiful woman, who had brought such comfort to so many—a woman who had so seldom cried in her life. Then her pastor opened the Bible and read those glorious words of Jesus, ". . . lo, I am with you always . . . . "

Although Corrie could not speak in sentences, she looked up, the blue eyes radiant once more, and said in a whisper, *"Always, always, always!"* The joy returned, she knew that Jesus had not deserted her—He was right there with her, and the triumphant spirit shone from His Corrie once more.

Friends would come to see her and they would hear her pray in her native Dutch tongue—the learned foreign language had left her—but as she spoke of her Lord, there was an understanding that surpassed language barriers. Her face would shine with the love of Christ, as she spoke of Him.

Hans Moolenburgh, Corrie's doctor from Holland, visited her and afterwards made these comments in *The Hiding Place* magazine:

> When you think about Tante Corrie, stop thinking of a helpless or childlike person, or even an empty shell. Think of a beautiful, old

lady shedding light, as if a hidden lighthouse shines from within. Think about a generous, fun-loving, prayerful, and very wise lady, who has retained all the majesty that makes several people spontaneously greet her with "Hello, Queen!"

Please rejoice with us and with Tante Corrie, for she is hid in His strength and only joy remains!

Corrie is greeted by Cliff Barrows, master of ceremonies for the program.

Hans Poley, with his wife, Mies, and Corrie remember the days in the Beje during the war.

Peter van Woerden talks with Corrie and Cliff Barrows.

Lotte Reimeringer talks of the rehabilitation center Corrie set up for refugees after the war.

Evie Tournquist sings for Corrie.

The Bill Gaither Trio sings of God's goodness.

George Beverly Shea sings a favorite of Corrie's: "How Great Thou Art!"

Jeannette Clift recalls for Corrie an amusing incident from the filming of THE HIDING PLACE.

Joni Eareckson and Corrie, with Carole Carlson in the background.

Corrie jubilant, as she wears the Indian headdress previously given to her when she was made a member of the Indian tribes.

"My son, Do," as Corrie calls Pastor Do Van Nguyen from Vietnam.

Ruth Graham looks on as Corrie receives a call from Billy Graham.

Bill Brown of World Wide Pictures and Bill Barbour of Revell Company share a happy moment with Corrie.

Duane Pederson, Bettie and Bill Butler listen as Corrie talks of their ministry together.

Corrie looks at a smaller copy of the life-size portrait of herself, presented by Mary Crowley. Joni Eareckson, Gloria Gaither, and Ruth Graham look on.

Beth Brain, stewardess, flew in from Minneapolis to express appreciation to Corrie for leading her to Christ.

Corrie with the bouquet presented to her by Billie Barrows (extreme right). Applauding are Carole Carlson, Edgar and Thelma Elfstrom.

Corrie is given a standing ovation in Denver. She often says, "In America, I receive so much praise, the halo gets so heavy on my head."

"I want each tribute to represent a beautiful flower."

"At night I collect them into a bouquet and say, 'Here, Lord, they belong to You!'"

13
Happy Birthday

Joan Winmill Brown reads birthday messages.

Corrie was born on Good Friday 1892 and her eighty-seventh birthday fell on Easter Sunday 1979. Friends from all over the world wrote to her—Shalom was filled with beautiful floral arrangements. It was a joyous day for Corrie, as greetings sent by so many were read to her. Those sending greetings included Billy and Ruth Graham, Joni Eareckson, Oral and Evelyn Roberts, and scores of others. Catherine Marshall wrote:

> How appropriate it is that you are going to have your eighty-seventh birthday on Easter Sunday. We rejoice over the great ministry a loving heavenly Father has given you over so many years. . . .
>
> We love you, Corrie; know that God spared you and brought you out of the concentration camp for His own purposes; praise Him that the message of love, even for our enemies, and the Christian

142

reconciliation made possible through Christ between all men has blessed thousands and thousands around the world, and will continue to do so . . . .

Bill and Vonette Bright of Campus Crusade for Christ International sent greetings:

> . . . . the world is a better place in which to live because God sent you to share His love and forgiveness in Jesus Christ. You are always a tremendous source of inspiration . . . .

With the greetings came recollections of amusing incidents, cherished memories. Carole Carlson told Tante Corrie she felt her life had been changed while working with her on *In My Father's House*. At first Carole had been rather in awe of Corrie, but as the days went by, working closely with her, she saw Corrie's sense of humor, her indomitable spirit. Carole gave one example:

> One day in front of your home in Overveen, Holland, I saw you in action. Our car was parked across the street. Julianalaan is a very busy thoroughfare, with cars and bicycles whizzing by without regard to speed laws. We walked to the edge of the road and waited for the stream of cars to ease, so we could cross. I had my hand on your arm, protectively. We stood and stood.
> Finally, with a tug of your arm away from mine, you thrust into the street and said, "Come . . . . we go!" Cars screeched and honked, as we marched across to our waiting car.
> It whizzed through my mind: *After all she has been through, this would be a very ignoble way to die!* Since that time, whenever there are obstacles in our path and indecision wavers our thinking, we have a family saying. It is:"Come . . . we go!"

Fran Ewing of Valparaiso, Florida, wrote, recalling when Corrie's life had touched her and her husband, Mike, so deeply. It was the first time they met:

> You took Mike's and my hands into yours and looked up to heaven and prayed a prayer that opened heaven to us. I had never before met

a person transparent enough to permit me to see Jesus, but as you prayed I saw Him and loved Him with a heart bursting with love. I gave Him my heart and never in all these years have I regretted the decision I made that day.

Bill and Isabelle Middendorf sent greetings. While he was United States Ambassador to Holland, Bill had been led to Christ by Corrie with the help of Bill's wife, Isabelle, and his minister, John Lewis. Bill wrote:

At the embassy I recall your wonderful witness to the Russian Ambassador, who always told me Christ's death on the cross was a stupid act of futility—a waste. Your valiant efforts to correct this, and other misconceptions he had, seemed to have fallen on deaf ears; but no one can be exposed to your radiance, Corrie, for very long and not retain in the recesses of the mind a new Light for one's way. What a blessed spirit is yours, Corrie!

Isabelle Middendorf wrote to Corrie:

How we love you! The special times with you will always be cherished. You were so encouraging to me when I was quaking in my boots at the thought of being an ambassador's wife!

The other precious time was back in the States in McClean, Virginia, when you spoke to about twenty-nine ladies in our home. My husband was Secretary of the Navy then, so many were government wives. They heard the message of salvation very clearly. We will always be grateful to our beautiful sister in Jesus . . . I know you prayed for salvation for our family. We are all redeemed—praise God!

Roy Rogers and Dale Evans Rogers were among those sending birthday greetings. Dale wrote:

Our first meeting was in the Chapel in the Canyon, Canoga Park, California. As long as I live, I shall remember your face, alight with the Holy Spirit, as you unfolded your amazing account of His Grace, enabling you to love and bless your captors in that infamous concentration camp. This is the kind of love that turns the world sunny-side up instead of upside down.

This old world is infinitely richer with compassion because of your incredibly beautiful life in Jesus . . . A blessed eighty-seventh celebration!

One of your most ardent fans,

DALE EVANS ROGERS

Bill and Gloria Gaither wrote:

We at the Gaither house think of you often and pray God's blessing for you on this day, especially. We will never forget the time you spent with us, sharing at our table the wisdom that life has taught you. Our children will never be the same, for you have helped them to realize the importance of praising and trusting God in all circumstances, and the importance of backing up our verbal praise with total commitment that goes beyond mere lip service.

They also remember your wry, Dutch humor, and they giggle when they think of the way you shivered when you complained of how we Americans hug everybody—even strangers! But when we see you again, should we slip and hug you without thinking, it will not be a phony, social gesture; it will be genuine affection from a family whose lives you have touched and who love you in Jesus for your very self . . . . Happy Birthday!

Elisabeth Elliot, who has known the suffering of losing her husband when he was martyred for Christ in the Amazon, wrote:

It is true for both of us—'oft times He weaveth sorrow'—but your life is the very characteristic of joy. It shines. Many times from the platform I have spoken of you as an example of the great principle of the transfiguration of experience. Out of that unspeakable suffering has come unspeakable joy for thousands, the living, irrefutable proof that the Lord gives beauty for ashes. Thank you, Corrie, from my heart, for showing this to us all by the unarguable evidence of an exchanged life.

I know your birthday will be a happy one. The path of the just, the Bible tells us "'shineth more and more unto the Perfect Day."

Many lovely photographs were taken of Corrie on her eighty-seventh birthday, sitting in the garden surrounded by her flowers and birds. (One cheeky little baby sparrow, his feathers puffed out—oblivious of all the fuss of birthday cakes, floral tributes, and cards—went right on eating from the bird feeder Corrie loved to fill each day.

She watched him with a beautiful smile on her face, her eyes lit up with joy at the sight of this little creature, who unquestioningly ate the food provided for him. Doubtless it reminded her of the Lord's daily provision each day of her incredible life.)

Bob van Woerden, Peter's brother, wrote of his aunt shortly after her birthday:

> There is a photograph of Tante Corrie in front of me, taken on her eighty-seventh birthday: a face which even now reflects vitality, love of life, and a strong will. Things which have struck me and which could possibly add to the Corrie ten Boom phenomena are as follows:
>
> *Her sense of humor in her religious conversations and prayers never overstepped the mark.* She always retained a sensible attitude. In other words her religious life did not exclude laughter. It was, in fact, a distinguishing mark of it.
>
> *Her unconditional positive regard for everybody she met.* It seems to me that this was her strongest point. Through this she discovered possibilities in others, which had been hidden until then. This usually caused the people around her to "blossom"—they felt happier and freer, constantly stimulated by her continuous, warm interest. This characteristic was also lived out by her immediate family, all of whom were gifted by this exceptional trait.
>
> *The third characteristic is the fact that she remained herself under all circumstances and in all situations.* Her inner experience and her outward behavior did not contradict each other, but showed a great congruity. She always gave the true impression of being "transparent," which gave her message an exceptional authority.
>
> *Last, I want to point to her "empathy."* I have always been amazed at the extent to which this "spinster-tante" was able to place herself in the most strange lives. Distances were bridged between her and notorious criminals, prostitutes, and yes, even between her and a sometimes out-of-step nephew, BOB.

It was only a few weeks after Corrie's birthday that she suffered another stroke. Not so severe as the first, but, nevertheless, because of her age and the short time since her last stroke, it was a serious setback. Nurses were brought to Shalom to minister to her during the night and part of the day.

Ruthe Messenger, a close friend of Corrie and whose husband, Dr. David Messenger, has taken care of her during her illnesses, spoke of the wonderful way in which the Lord undertook even in using Corrie to silently witness to the nurses.

> They each remarked that it was not like work, caring for Corrie. It seemed as if they were in a sanctuary and the Lord was so close.
>
> For all of us it has been hard to see Corrie having to just lie in bed, but it has been a beautiful experience too. One night I went in to see her and was told she had not responded all day. It was my birthday, and Pam and Lotte had given me two presents. Corrie has always opened all of our gifts at Christmas and birthdays, as she loves to do this so much.
>
> I went over to her bed and said, "Corrie, I need your help. Please help me open my presents." There was a flicker of recognition, and gradually her left hand came up, and she put her fingers through the bow on the package and gently pulled the ribbon—helping me. I finished opening the package but she was not interested in the contents.
>
> Then I said to her, "Corrie, this is a bigger present; I need your help more than ever." Again she responded and helped me untie the bow. When I unwrapped it, inside I saw a beautiful photo of her taken on her birthday. I held it up to her and said, "Thank you, Corrie." Her eyes lit up, and she smiled her lovely smile, and then pointed to heaven. It was my most beautiful birthday present.

The goodness of God has been so evident through all the time that Corrie has been ill. When she has had to rely so completely on others, He has given her friends who have meant so much to her. Two such friends are Ronald Rietveld of California State University (Fullerton) and his wife, Ruth. Professor Rietveld, whose family were in the Dutch underground during the war, reflects on his impressions of Corrie:

> When I first met her, I shared about my family in Holland and how they had suffered in the war—I felt a real love and understanding from her. Because the Lord's presence in her is so real, it drew me to her. She was herself. She was authentic. She said how she felt, lovingly . . . but she would not bend. Her will was loving but strong. There is still a deep strength that attracts people.

Ruth Rietveld remembers the time Corrie came to speak to a Church History class at Talbot Theological Seminary (California), and the students listened, spellbound.

> She spoke for nearly an hour. When she finished she said, "Next time I'm asked to speak, I must wear more comfortable shoes—my feet are killing me!"
>
> Everyone feels as if she is family—a grandmother, mother, sister—people identify with her.

Two other friends who have unobtrusively helped in any way they could are Professor Vuryl Klassen, also of Cal State, and his wife, Jane. Gifts have been left on the doorstep of Shalom—food that they knew Corrie would like. Jane stitched pillows to help make her Dutch neighbor more comfortable during her time of illness. The Klassens' love for Corrie has grown over the months they have known her. It was the joy that she introduced into Jane's life that changed this young woman completely—Jane began to read Corrie's books and through them started seeking Jesus Christ.

Dr. Messenger, who has been Corrie's physician and friend since she settled in California, tells of meeting her when she spoke at Garden Grove Community Church:

> Dr. Robert Schuller was doing a series on "Being Persecuted for Righteousness Sake," and he invited Corrie to speak on this subject. Afterwards, my wife and I were introduced to Corrie, and later I had the opportunity to be of service to her with some of her continuing medical problems. When one of these necessitated hospitalizing her, she accepted the change in plans, canceling many speaking engagements with the calm serenity of the faith that "all things work together for good . . . ."

As her physician, Dr. Messenger has seen Corrie at some of the most painful moments in her life—moments that could easily have compromised her testimony—but always he has seen the inner strength that the Lord has given her. Even when two strokes felled her, making her unable to speak, he saw an aura of radiance coming from her: the radiance of Jesus.

With Catherine Marshall.

Vonette Bright, Corrie, and Bill Bright.

Corrie's "cheeky" baby sparrow,
who attended the birthday party.

Former Secretary of the Navy Bill Middendorf,
Corrie, and Isabelle Middendorf.

Corrie was a special guest on Dr. Robert Schuller's television program. From left
to right: Charles Colson, Dr. Schuller, Eldridge Cleaver, and Norma Zimmer.

14

Ministering Without Words

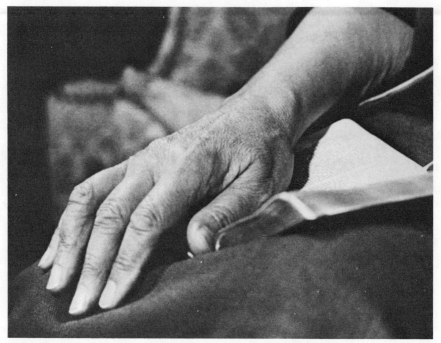

Corrie's hand rests on her Bible.

Why does Corrie have to suffer—not physical pain—but the day-by-day lingering here on earth, when all that she really wants is to be with Jesus?

Again the Lord showed the answer to the *whys*. Her sickroom became His place of consolation. A night nurse who had been so deeply troubled found unexpected comfort from the still, elderly lady who had been assigned to her care. The nurse saw the quiet radiance of Corrie and of those who came to visit her. There was a love and peace that she had not seen when caring for most of her other patients. Questioning Pamela and Lotte, she learned that it was Jesus Christ who made the difference.

Only a few weeks before in Shalom she had done just this. Aurelia Mojarro, who helps clean Corrie's home and had not known her before her two strokes, still saw the light of Christ in this stricken woman. In a holy and beautiful moment, she gave her life to the Lord in Corrie's living room. Pamela shared this glorious example of Jesus' love reaching out from Corrie: "I knew that Tante Corrie was much in prayer, as I talked with Aurelia, and she was very joyful when Aurelia went to her and told her that she had accepted the Lord Jesus Christ. 'Good . . . good,' said Tante Corrie, who looked really radiant. I knew that she wanted to say what she always used to say on such an occasion . . . 'There is joy in heaven. You have made the decision which the Bible tells us causes the angels to rejoice!' "

When people came to see Corrie after her second stroke, and they would begin to talk to her of Jesus, Corrie's eyes would become luminous with His love. A smile could be seen on her face. Earthly things did not matter to her anymore, only heavenly things.

> Turn your eyes upon Jesus,
> Look full in His wonderful face,
> And the things of earth will grow strangely dim,
> In the light of His glory and grace.

Lotte Reimeringer and Pamela have taken turns to be by Corrie's bedside. Their love for her has been so evident, and it has been silently and glowingly returned by Corrie. Pamela reflects on what it has been like to work with and take care of her:

Right from the beginning Tante Corrie has shared all aspects of her ministry and life with me. She has never had secrets or complicated ways of dealing with things. Since she is so close to the Lord Jesus, working with her has meant getting to know Him better—learning how to serve. That is a daily learning process and though I still have far to go, I can really say that serving is the very highest calling, because it means real identification with Jesus Christ.

With Tante Corrie's two strokes, our way of life changed radically, since she was no longer able to communicate through speech or writing. I believe that Satan tried to deal a deathblow to her life's message that Jesus Christ was, is, and will be Victor. However, instead, God used it for good. I had always seen the Lord Jesus in Tante Corrie, but in her physical weakness I see Him so much more clearly.

She is always pointing Lotte and me to Him—before her second stroke sometimes literally with her hand, as she would indicate to heaven and say with a radiant face, "I cannot . . . but He . . . He can!" At all times in her life I have seen the wonderful fruit of the Holy Spirit—peace, patience, joy, love, kindness, goodness, faithfulness, gentleness, self-control. I am reminded of Hebrews 12:11 [NAS]:

> All discipline for the moment seems not to be joyful,
> but sorrowful; yet to those who have been trained by
> it, afterwards it yields the peaceful fruit of righteous-
> ness.

There is a ripe and peaceful fruit of righteousness visible in Tante Corrie's life. It is a victory of the Lord Jesus.

Taking care of Corrie has meant a continuing, beautiful experience in friendship in the life of Lotte Reimeringer—who exemplifies true kindness. She says:

> When I arrived here in December 1978, it was wanting to do what my hands would find to do and every bit of this has been full of the joy and peace of the Lord. Being with Tante Corrie and seeing what God is able to do in the life of a child of His—that each new day gives everything completely into His hands, desiring His will to be done, whatever this may mean to the human side—it just causes me to worship His greatness.
>
> In Tante Corrie, God has in a special way demonstrated during these months that His way *is* perfect and that His strength *is* made perfect in weakness. Tante Corrie is not some "superbeing"—she is a child of the All-Sufficient One who is proving His all-sufficiency time again in the varying everyday circumstances.
>
> It is His love we see shining through her, *His* peace, *His* grace . . . In dark moments, He says to her, "Fear not, I am here, I am holding your right hand." To see the outworking of this is the wonderful thing of being allowed to take care of Tante Corrie.

Through her life Corrie has not been a "superbeing," as Lotte said. But she is a perfect example of the way in which God can use a life that is *completely* surrendered to Him.

When people would say to Corrie, "I wish I had your faith," she was quick to respond to them. A neighbor of hers in Haarlem once said to her, when she returned from Ravensbruck, "I am sure it was your faith that helped you through."

Corrie answered, "*My* faith? I don't know. My faith was so weak, so wavering, sometimes it was difficult to believe. When everything is safe around you, it is easy. But in a camp, where you saw your own sister and thousands of others starve, where people who had had training in cruelties surrounded us, I don't know if my faith helped me through. No, it was Jesus! He who said, 'I am with you always, 'til the end of the world.' It was *His* everlasting arms underneath me that carried me through. He was my security.

"If I say it was *my* faith, then you, whenever you have to pass through hardships, can say, 'I have not Corrie's faith.' But when I tell you it was *Jesus,* then you can trust that the same One who has carried me through will do the same for you. I have always believed—now I know!"

In her talks Corrie would often quote this poem:

> Coward and wayward and weak,
> I change with the changing sky,
> Today so eager and brave—
> Tomorrow not caring to try.
> But *He* never gives in—
> And we two shall win,
> Jesus and I!

Whenever Corrie would prepare a message, she would ask the Lord to guide her and, "Please, Lord, give me a little humor!" He always did—the audiences loved to see the twinkle and the surprised look on Corrie's face, as she made a point with a joke, only to drive home in the next sentence a profound truth of the Lord's.

Once she told an audience, "You know, when I have spoken and the

Lord used me, sometimes not even afterwards, but *during* the time I am speaking, the devil says to me, 'You do a good job today,' and then I say '*Shut up!*' It is not the power of *my* mouth, but the *Holy Spirit,* and when it is not the Holy Spirit, we can have brilliant meetings, but there is no blessing at all.''

As she reread her messages, she would always say, ''But is the *cross* in there?'' If it were not clearly presented, back she would go and rewrite, until it had pre-eminence. She would repeat to her audience:

> At the cross, at the cross,
> Where I first saw the Light
> And the *burden* of my heart rolled away,
> It was there by faith I received my sight.
>   ISAAC WATTS

The forgiveness and love of Jesus Christ have flooded Corrie's life. When she returned from Ravensbruck, from all the hell and sorrow she had faced, Jesus gave her forgiveness for her enemies. Even when the very man who had betrayed the ten Booms was caught after the war, and sentenced to die, Corrie wrote him a letter, telling him that she forgave what he did to her and her family. She wrote:

> . . . The harm you planned was turned into good for me by God. I came nearer to Him. A severe punishment is waiting you. I have prayed for you . . . the Lord will accept you, if you will repent. Think that the Lord Jesus on the cross also took your sins upon Himself. If you accept this and want to be *His* child, you are saved for eternity.
>
> I have forgiven you everything. God will also forgive you everything, if you ask Him.

People have asked Corrie how she could forgive and love her enemies—those who let her father and Betsie die. She has answered, ''It is the love that the Holy Spirit gives. You never touch the ocean of God's love, as when you love your enemies. The Lord Jesus has shown us His obedience to the Father, and we have to follow Him. The sweetest commandment in the Bible is, 'Be filled with the Spirit.' It is a *commandment*—it is not a suggestion. Jesus is the door—it is Jesus who baptizes with the Holy Spirit. He will keep you steadfast in the faith to the end. He will give you power!"

When people meet Corrie they are always struck by the radiance of her twinkling blue eyes. Her hands, too—so impressive—as she would use them to express a point. Many have found themselves thinking, *"These are the hands that mended watches; that endured the concentration camp; that touched little children and brought the love of Jesus to them, so that they could grow into beautiful, caring human beings.*

Her hands rest on her Bible, as each day she seeks the Lord's guidance, comfort, and wisdom. How Corrie has always known the importance of being in close contact with Him through His Word! She has said, "When our family was arrested during the war, my nephew Peter came to me and said, 'Tante Corrie, what have you in your shoe?' I said, 'Romans Eight. What have you?' He said, 'I have Ephesians One.' Do you realize what was happening? We were going to a place where it was possible that our Bibles would be taken away. They took away my Romans Eight, but there was something they could not take away: that was all the verses I had learned by heart. *Learn by heart the verses of the Bible.* It will be a help when tribulation comes. There is so much in the Bible that gives us ammunition for the battle. The Holy Spirit can teach you what verses you must learn by heart."

If Corrie could speak to us today, concerning the world situation, she would probably repeat what she told audiences all over the world:

> Do not be afraid! Through the darkness of now:
> "Look around and be distressed—
> Look within and be depressed—
> Look at Jesus and be at rest!"

Do you sometimes get frightened when you read in the Bible all the things that are happening right now in the world? If I never believed in the Bible before, I would now! Read the newspaper, and it can make you scared, because there are things happening that the Bible has already told us about—terrible things!

Read the Book of Revelation. When you are afraid, read the last pages! *Hallelujah!* It is written on the last pages that Jesus has said, "I will come back and I will make everything new!"

That is the future! You stand in the front line of the battle that *will* have victory, because Jesus will be Victor and He will make you more than conquerors. Betsie was sick and weak, but she placed her hand in the hand of the strong One—Jesus.

If I must die before Jesus returns, that is also good. Death, for a child of God, is not a pit but a tunnel to go through to the great joy of heaven. I know one thing—*the best is yet to be*. Not only for me—for God has loved the world so much "that He sent His only begotten Son that whosoever believes in Him will not perish but have everlasting life." There will come a time when I will have to die. How good to know that I belong to Jesus.

Do you know it? If not, lay your hand in His strong hand. What a joy!

Corrie's Papa would often say to her: "When Jesus takes your hand, He keeps it tight. When He keeps it tight, He leads you through life. And when He leads you through life, He brings you safely home."

Only a few more steps and Corrie will be safely home with the One who has walked each day with her. Jesus will welcome her into her heavenly home. What reunions there will be: Papa, Mama, Betsie, and all her loved ones that have gone before! It is hard to begin to imagine all the preparations that will have been made for her arrival.

> Eye hath not seen, nor ear heard, neither have entered into the heart of man, the things which God hath prepared for them that love him.
>
> 1 Corinthians 2:9 KJV

Corrie would sometimes quote:

> When I enter that beautiful city,
> And the saved all around me appear,
> I hope that someone will tell me,
> "It was *you* who invited me here."

Look back on the influence of the life of this child whose earthly father prayed that the little "grain of wheat" might bear much fruit for the kingdom of God! In heaven she will be met by *so many* who will say, "Corrie, it was *you* who invited me here!"

The lives Corrie has touched and will continue to touch until Jesus comes cannot be counted here on this earth.

But one day . . . !

In the garden of Shalom, Corrie enjoys her "quiet time" with the Lord.

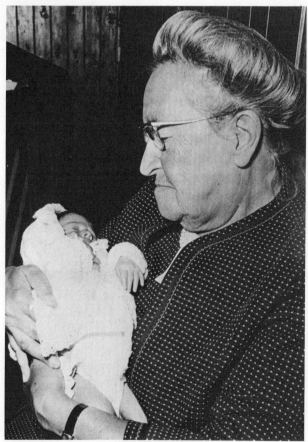

Age and youth.

"Do not be afraid . . . read the last pages of the Bible: Jesus is Victor!"

Index